FOREWORD

As your read this guidebook you will begin to realise that Glasgow has had the most remarkable and epochal relationship with the architecture and the power of the industrial revolution. Many of the city's most compelling buildings can only be really understood in relationship to social change. For decades it seemed that Glasgow was stuck in the past – but the forces of change propelled it forward again as the regenerative powers of post-industrialism turned Glasgow into a city with a formidable identity in the arts, design, new technology and consumerism.

Glasgow is an extraordinary city and although I love it, I was not born here and had already studied in New York and London before I settled here. My first real contact with its architecture was tentative and uninformed. I remember that a few months after I arrived in the city, a friend gave me a cherished piece of advice. Take ten minutes every day to look up. Look above the shops, look above the eye-line and look beyond the first floor of the buildings you are walking past.

Look up and you will see something compelling. It might be small at first and seemingly inconsequential. By the time the day is over you will have caught glimpses and side-views of literally hundreds of architectural moods and influences from medieval pastiche to post-modernism.

You will know that you are in a city that has had a unique dialogue with the history of architecture. Then you can wake up the next day and begin to enjoy the city.

Stuart Cosgrove

Stuart Cosgrove
Head of Programmes, Channel 4

© Johnny Rodger 1999
Series editor: Charles McKean
Editorial consultant: Duncan McAra
Index: Oula Jones

The Rutland Press
ISBN 1 873190 51 4

Cover illustrations
Front main Detail, Clyde Auditorium, SECC (Richard Davies) *Insert left* Princes House (Alan McAteer) *Insert right* Tontine heads, St Nicholas Garden (Gary Johnson) *Back left to right* Institute of Health Sciences (Keith Hunter) Berkeley Square (Andrew Lee) William Harley Library (Austin Smith : Lord) Tontine head, St Nicholas Garden (Gary Johnson)

Designed and Produced by The Almond Consultancy, Edinburgh
Printed by Nimmos Colour Printers, Edinburgh

fionasinclair.architect

studio 17, sir james clark building
abbey mill business centre paisley PA1 1TJ
tel: 0141-848 6766 fax: 0141-889 8890

The Rutland Press gratefully acknowledges
the generous support of MacRoberts
Solicitors in producing this guide.
We also thank the following practices whose
assistance secured the project: Glass Murray
Architects; Keppie Architects; Page & Park

Glass Murray
architects

Drummond House
1 Hill Street
Glasgow
G3 6BN

Tel: 0141 331 2926
Fax: 0141 332 6790

PAGE & PARK ARCHITECTS

Italian Centre, 49 Cochrane Street, Glasgow G1 1HL
Tel: 0141 552 0686 Fax: 0141 552 1466

Architects; The Parr Partnership; Fiona
Sinclair, Architect; 3D Architects;
Anderson Christie Architects; Boswell
Mitchell & Johnston; Building Design
Partnership; The Carl Fisher Sibbald
Partnership; Crerar & Partners; Davis

THE
PARR
PARTNERSHIP

A R C H I T E C T S

8 NEWTON PLACE
GLASGOW G37PR
TEL: 0141 331 2644 FAX: 0141 333371
EMAIL: PARRGLASGOW@COMPUSERVE.COM

GLASGOW

EDINBURGH

PERTH

LONDON

DUBLIN

Keppie ARCHITECTS
Architects, Planners and Designers

Duncan Harrold; Elder and Cannon
Architects; Holmes Partnership; McKeown
Alexander Architects; Reiach and Hall
Architects; RMJM Scotland Ltd; Vernon
Monaghan Architects; Wren Rutherford
ASL; Zoo Architects.

**GLASGOW INSTITUTE
OF ARCHITECTS**

The Glasgow Institute of
Architects is one of the six
regional chapters of the RIAS
and has been in existence since
1858. Its council of elected
members seeks to serve and
promote the profession in the
Glasgow area. It organises
activities which raise public
consciousness of the art of
architecture, and which create
an opportunity for fellowship
within the profession.

CITY OF REGENERATION?

In this book's companion volume *Central Glasgow* Charles McKean describes the history of this city in a way which might be summed up metaphorically as the diastole/systole movement of a great urban heart: the boom-to-bust, in turn, of its ecclesiastical, mercantile and industrial eras. The latter movement, the industrial age, is figured to end around 1910 with the exhaustion of the coal and ore fields in Glasgow's hinterland. Only the shock of the two World Wars, it is said, and the resulting temporary stimulation of the shipbuilding and munitions industries kept the old heart ticking over into the mid-decades of this century. The question, for this guide, is, where is Glasgow now in terms of this cyclical movement, and what, architecturally

speaking, are its symptoms? Is it still stuttering on to the end of its industrial bust, or has a new boom era already begun? There have been many claims that a 'regeneration' of this city is currently under way. What is the evidence?

In Scotland, as with the rest of the Western World, the breakdown of the modernist project – that great programme of social works: housing, hospitals, schools – was precipitated in the early 1970s by the oil crisis. Modernism and the state planning that had dominated the construction world since the Second World War, along with its orthodox no-frills style of

functionalism, was engulfed in a wave of disillusion. Centrally controlled 'progress' gained a reputation in some quarters for being dull and oppressive. In 1976 the seventh new town project for overspill from Glasgow to be sited in Stonehouse was cancelled and the funds redirected into Glasgow East Area Renewal (GEAR). Some time before this Assist Architects had started a programme in the city to rehabilitate the tenement, a traditional building much despised by modernists. At the end of the decade a British Government with a radical manifesto for movement away from the consensus politics and government planning

INTRODUCTION

of the post-war period towards individualism and *laissez-faire* economics came to power. Despite the unpopularity of this government in Scotland, and its perceived attacks on the nation's social cohesion, it had much 'success' with the introduction of its policies and the social, political, economic and cultural face of the country was, throughout the 1980s, changed irretrievably.

It was in the 1980s that the concept 'regeneration' first started to be used with respect to the city. They were all post-modernists in Glasgow now: along with the abandonment of plans for new towns and outlying housing schemes, and the switch from slum clearance programmes to tenement rehabilitation, came a concentration on rebuilding the urban fabric. As Miles Glendinning *et al* say in *The History of Scottish Architecture*: 'Scotland participated avidly in a new and vigorous international movement – Post-modernism.' Going on to define the post-modern characteristics of this architecture in the 1980s the same authors highlight: 'A growing emphasis on decoration, eclectic appearance and façades' and 'emphasis on piecemeal interventions and mixed uses, following patterns and context established by existing old buildings, reflecting "the city in its contradictory and even chaotic essence"'.

Above Carrick Quay (Anne Dick)
Right Italian Centre Courtyard (Keith Hunter)
Opposite Shakespeare Street Housing *above* site plan *below* elevation to street (MLDO Architects)

2

The finest example of this new post-modern urbanism is to be found in the so-called **Merchant City**. This area west of the High Street and north of the Trongate was originally settled in the 18th century as a new town by rich merchants who had made new money in the Americas. As the city spread westwards up Blythswood Hill the merchants moved on and the area was built up with warehouses and offices around the central markets. By the 1970s these markets had closed down and much of the warehouse and office property was pretty down-at-heel if not derelict. The new urbanism of the 1980s, however, meant that money was invested in the development of inner cities, and there was a policy of introducing new housing, boutiques, cafés and bars to this area through both conversion of the existing stock of warehouses, and 'sympathetic' new-build.

Two particular schemes were front runners in the development that took place during this period: **Ingram Square** by Elder and Cannon Architects, and **The Italian Centre** by Page & Park Architects. Inasmuch as both these schemes consisted of single urban warehouse blocks/squares developed into housing, office and retail units by an individual architectural practice, they reflect the 'piecemeal' basis – involving many architects and many different types of 'intervention'– in which this work was carried out. Also typical of the post-modern approach was the attention paid in both these schemes to decoration, the façades and 'fun'; thus in Ingram Square with its corner glass drums, its stylised pediments, gables and

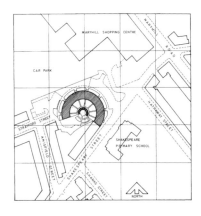

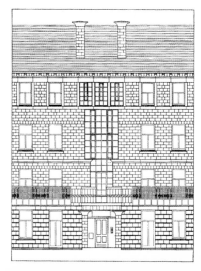

Introduction

balconets, and The Italian Centre with its effusion of sculpture, of metalwork balconies, sunshades and shutters, and bands of coloured stone. It is important also that both schemes took care with rehabilitation of the courtyards, which in Glasgow were formerly used only for dumping household rubbish. In this way a private urban realm was created as an alternative to a suburban garden.

If it is not surprising that as a reaction to the austerity of the modernist programme there was in the 1980s an

embracing of a sort of fickle neo-classicism, and a nostalgia for the life and forms of the pre-industrial city (remembering that the Merchant City has its origins in the 18th century) then what is quite unexpected is that in the following decade – that with which we are directly concerned – there is a reaction in turn against these, relatively new post-modern forms. All of a sudden, in the 1990s the standard post-modern approach, that vigorous frenzy of neo-classical details, which seemed once, by way of Leon Krier and James Stirling and others, to bring liberation

from a modernist totalitarianism, now appeared simply confused, cheap and tacky. There was a return to a limited idealism, to a respect for autonomous form, which is reflected in the Davis Duncan Partnership's comment on their **Carrick Quay** building (first phase completed in 1989, work underway 1998): 'there is no place here for the panoply of applied decoration exhibited by the Postmodern. The building is unashamedly modern, expressing the spirit of a society in the 1990s.'

Throughout this decade 1989-99, however, notwithstanding the evident abandonment of the post-modern approach, the claims that Glasgow is undergoing a 'regeneration' have not abated. In fact they have become more frenzied, almost to the point where the concept 'regeneration' has taken on the value of a 'credo' amongst Glaswegians. Unfortunately, not all the citizens are of the faith. In this new religious divide amongst Glaswegians the infidels have been characterised as 'misfits, dilettanti, well-heeled authors and critics; professional whingers, crypto-communists, self-proclaimed anarchists, trotskyists' (from a 10,000-word document by the one-time leader of Glasgow City Council, and Lord Provost, Pat Lally, quoted in *Some Recent Attacks* by James Kelman) and 'the po-faced protestations of certain cynics prophesying economic ruin and moral decay' (from an article in *Prospect* by the architect Nicholas Groves-Raines about his **Saltmarket** development). What are we to make of these shrill denunciations by the proponents of the idea of 'regeneration'? Why are they so touchy?

Above Annandale Square Housing (Keith Hunter)

INTRODUCTION

Even the agnostic observer, however, as he or she looks on at this crusade, must admit that the type of symptom typically supposed to denote the existence of 'regeneration' has proliferated within the period in question.

First, there has been an attempt to fashion Glasgow as the city of festivals, to find success as a post-industrial city by forcing the association of the city's name away from one of smoke, dirt, poverty, toughness and industry towards a new one of culture, cosmopolitanism, entertainment, art, style and design. Key concepts in this change have been the importance locally and internationally of the work of architect C R Mackintosh and the integration of the 'spirit' of his work into the supposed cosmopolitan ethos of a city most of whose

inhabitants live (as in all cities in Scotland), continental-style, in blocks of flats. The promotion of this new image has been fired by the attraction to the city of major international festivals. In 1988 **The Glasgow Garden Festival** was held in a disused dockyard; a year-long cultural extravaganza was held as **Cultural Capital of Europe** in 1990, and in 1999 Glasgow takes pride in the accolade **UK City of Architecture and Design**. The two former festivals pushed the idea of Glasgow as a city which had recovered its true heritage from the ravages of its industrial recent past, and the latter is seemingly concerned with the renaissance of the city through architectural culture.

Another factor cited in this 'regeneration' has been the work of the housing associations. Since the monolithic

Right Bellgrove Street Housing *above* by day *below* by night (Keith Hunter)

regional housing authorities started to be broken up into 'community-based' associations in the 1970s they had been carrying out rehabilitation of the 19th-century housing stock. By the end of the 1980s this rehabilitation was almost complete and the associations were turning their attention towards new-build on gap sites, and urban infill. Thanks to promotion of new private/public initiatives by the then government, these housing associations were in a position to become patrons of the development of new tenement design. Several awards were set up for such designs, and throughout the period such award-winning schemes were built as:

• **Shakespeare Street Housing**, 1984-9, MLDO with Ken Macrae, for Maryhill Housing Association

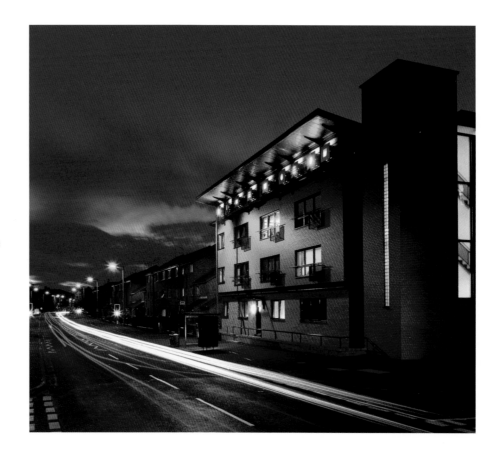

Above Dumbarton Road Housing (Andrew Lee)

- **Duke Street Housing**, 1992, Elder and Cannon, for Reidvale Housing Association
- **Annandale Square**, 1994, Elder and Cannon, Govanhill Housing Association
- **Byres Road/University Avenue Housing**, 1994, Simister Monaghan, Hillhead Housing Association
- **Bellgrove Street Housing**, 1996, McGurn, for Molendinar Housing Association
- **Dumbarton Road Housing**, 1998, Anderson Christie, for Whiteinch Scotstoun Housing Association.

In a certain sense the culmination of this nurturing of tenement design has come with the **Crown Street Project** in Gorbals where a whole inner city area, formerly built up with modernist blocks (now demolished) is being comprehensively rebuilt in a mixed private/public development on the original street grid pattern with tenement housing designed by numerous different architectural practices.

Since the mid-1990s National Lottery money and the Millennium Fund have also become important sources for the funding of new buildings. As the lottery fund makes its resources available to capital projects in the 'cultural' field, this source has been much exploited in the push towards the creation of the new 'image' for Glasgow. Among the projects part funded in this way are the redevelopment of the **Tron Theatre**, by RMJM Scotland Ltd; the **Lighthouse**, a new architectural centre built as part of the 1999 Festival by Page & Park Architects; and the **Science Park** designed by Building Design Partnership. Other plans such as the extension of the **Arches Theatre** out from under **Central Station** to the *Hielanman's Umbrella* have received funding but not yet gone on site, and others still, like the planned National Gallery of Scottish Art and Design in the old George Square Post Office building, failed simply because they did not receive the required funding from these sources.

In terms specifically of architectural culture two other factors have a certain significance in this 'regeneration'. First, there is the central role which the two

Right Tron Theatre, detail of Chisholm Street elevation (Andrew Lee)
Opposite above Drawing of the Telefonica building, Barcelona (Colin Begg)
Opposite below Moffat Gardens (David Churchill)

8

schools of architecture, the Mackintosh at Glasgow School of Art, and the school at the University of Strathclyde, have played in the culture of the city. The schools were headed for a number of years by individuals of great energy and reputation within the profession, namely Professor Andy MacMillan and Professor Frank Walker at the Mackintosh and Strathclyde respectively. Evidence of the international dimension of their reputation is brought home by the number of foreign students attracted to these schools, and again by simple facts such as the Italian architecture magazine *Lotus* (issue No 73) featuring the Mackintosh in an article about the best architecture schools in Europe. What is vital about their teaching method is not only that they demand the level of

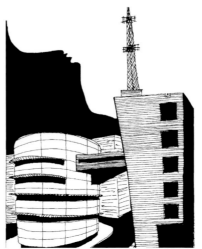

eclecticism and establishment of precedent usual in any architectural education but that this openness to influence is in turn focused on, and anchored firmly in practice in Glasgow. One English visiting external examiner was even led to complain that there was too much concentration on tenement-style building!

The fact that Assist Architects, the first to promote the rehabilitation of the tenement in the 1970s, had been students of the University of Strathclyde says something about the commitment to this city, but one tangible and more recent illustration of the effect of these methods can be seen in the geometric monumentality of the **Moffat Gardens tower** by Elder and Cannon. Most of the young designers in this firm were educated at the Mackintosh and quite a few of them tutor there. It is not too far-fetched to suggest that the plan of this building

might have been influenced by that of the Telefonica telephone exchange building in Barcelona by Nuñez & Mora, and the oversailing elliptical copper roof certainly has echoes of an installation designed by Carlo Scarpa for the Venice Biennale in 1952. Yet here it is, the Moffat Gardens tower building, centrepiece in a council estate in the Gorbals. (It is also true that much of the credit for the development of this building must be given to the enlightened patronage of Fraser Stewart, director of New Gorbals Housing Association.)

Together with the educational work of the schools has been the energetic promotion of architectural culture by The Royal Incorporation of Architects in Scotland throughout this period. Charles

McKean, now Professor of Scottish Architectural History at the University of Dundee, was head of the RIAS until 1995; he became an enthusiastic talking head on both television and radio, and launched such initiatives as this series of guides, the Regeneration Awards, and the opening of a second RIAS architectural bookshop, now at the Mackintosh School of Architecture, Scott Street, Glasgow, where knowledgeable staff provide a broad spectrum of the world of architecture, bringing in publications from all over Europe and America which otherwise would not be available in the city.

Armed with such powerful, persuasive and seemingly ubiquitous evidence as all that listed above, what, the innocent agnostic might ask, does it behove Messrs Lally and Groves-Raines, and other

proponents of 'regeneration', to be so touchy? If we agree that of all the above listed 'symptoms' the council-driven attempt to forge a new post-industrial image of the city, in particular as a city of cultural festivals, has been the most important, then it has also been the most problematic. The biggest of these festivals – the Year of Cultural Capital of Europe 1990 – allegedly cost the city around £50m, and its centrepiece, the **Glasgow's Glasgow** exhibition alone lost a figure variously reported as being between £3m and £10m. Mr Lally commented on this specific loss saying that the city had 'bought a lemon'. But the question must be, who paid for the lemon? By 1997 the city was near bankruptcy, council tax rises have been far higher in Glasgow than anywhere else in

Scotland for consecutive years, and there have been massive cuts in council services including the shutting down of day-centres, leisure facilities and libraries. Meanwhile, fixed to a wall on the building opposite Nicholas Groves-Raines' **Saltmarket** development in the centre of ancient Glasgow is a sign reading *Warning – these flats & garages are patrolled 24 hours per day*. It all starts to sound a bit more like disinheritance rather than regeneration.

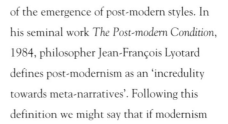

There is, however, no way of proving a 'regeneration' either way unless it be clearly established what is meant by that term. It is notable that 'regeneration' first began to be used as a description for what was happening in the city during the 1980s, just at the time of the emergence of post-modern styles. In his seminal work *The Post-modern Condition*, 1984, philosopher Jean-François Lyotard defines post-modernism as an 'incredulity towards meta-narratives'. Following this definition we might say that if modernism itself was historically a part of the Enlightenment, a movement of an all-encompassing (some might say Marxian, or even totalitarian) attempt to provide controlled progress, that is to understand, for example, the boom-and-bust cycles of the capitalist economic system, and through certain programmes to avoid them, or provide a cushion against them, then post-modernism is a rejection of the possibility of such understanding and legitimation. Thus the operation of post-modernism is 'piecemeal' (as Glendinning *et al* say) not just in terms of its decorative manifestation on architectural façades, but in essence. Just so, the whole notion of 'regeneration' seems to be a paradigm of that post-modernism. For is the concept 'regeneration' not an eternal seeking after 'boom' without any analysis given to its relationship to 'bust', which the meta-narrative called enlightened history would tell us will surely follow?

Might not this 'piecemeal' approach of 'regeneration' be dangerous for the cohesion of the city, especially if it concentrates its attention on the urban to the expense of the civic? It is fine to talk about historical 'busts' in terms of cities shrinking and new buildings no longer appearing, but what is behind the cuts in council services and the attempted exclusion of citizens from certain areas (see above) but human suffering? As regards the 'bust' of Glasgow's industrial period, which has lasted most of this century, it is estimated that more than 20,000 people have suffered from asbestosis directly as a result of shipyards attempting to cut costs.

All of which brings us, somewhat tardily it must be said, to the issue of 'the people'. There is surely some significance in the fact that throughout the period of this 'regeneration' the population of Greater Glasgow has been falling dramatically. If it is thus true that 'regeneration' concentrates its efforts on the city as urban (i.e. the aggregation of construction) as opposed to the city as civic (i.e. the aggregation of citizens), and so reproduces, one might say, certain late 19th- and early 20th-century attitudes of those in control, then the citizens themselves seem to answer with a corresponding disregard for the urban

environment. There is, in fact, a special quality of 'opposition', peculiar to Glasgow, when it comes to the relationship between 'buildings' and the 'people'.

Testimony to this notion as commonplace can be found in the Glasgow Tourist Board's promotional video in its George Square office (see p.50) where Cardinal Winning, spiritual leader of Glasgow's and Scotland's Roman Catholics, says that Glasgow is the people and not the buildings, and also from 'Radical Glasgow', an exhibition recently shown at the Mitchell Library, which stated 'Glasgow's heritage is more important than bricks and mortar.' More space needs to be given to analysis of this phenomenon than is available here, but let it just be said for now that the shibboleth-type nature of this utterance is hardly surprising on the lips of

a population whose city has, in the 20th century, boasted some of the worst slums in Europe. What makes it even less surprising, however, during this current period of 'regeneration' are some of the clumsy attempts that have been made to overcome this alienation of the people.

It is here that one specifically Glaswegian version of the post-modern styles – sometimes referred to by the derogatory term *Mockintosh* – is important. While clearly Charles Rennie Mackintosh invented neither the oriel window, nor, indeed, the square, the number of buildings designed in this city over the last 20 years with a certain type of gridded fenestration, similar in detail to the long windows on the west side of Mackintosh's Glasgow School of Art, is astonishing. The reader need only take a walk 60 yards along Cadogan Street in the 'business district' on the southern slopes of Blythswood Hill to find four massive office blocks, **Corunna House**, **Fitzpatrick House**, **Richmond Exchange** and **Pacific House**, each in an ostensibly different style, be it brickwork façade, modern glass curtain block or post-modern bands of coloured stone and pediments, but yet, each sporting the vertically orientated, gridded boxes of *Mockintosh* windows. What is the intention here – is it that these details should help the buildings in this business ghetto somehow to ingratiate themselves with the people and 'culture' of this city, or that they should thereby attain a Glasgow 'personality' and blend instantly with the cityscape? Personality or not, they have nothing of the aura of Mackintosh's originals and it is in some way only too appropriate that this business district, brazenly thrusting

its oriels in our faces by day, should become the red-light zone at night.

On the other hand, it might also be said that there is evidence that the 'people's' attitude to architecture and building in Glasgow is shifting. In 1993 DoCoMoMo (Documentation and Conservation of the Modern Movement) Scotland held a conference and series of seminars in Glasgow to discuss the modernist architectural heritage of this country. David Page of Page & Park Architects said in his contribution to that programme: 'Within the framework of continuity, it becomes less important to argue about whether the past was better or worse, about whether – for instance – Modernism was a utopia or a dystopia. What matters is simply that our choices should be properly informed by, should interact with, the past.'

Only with this type of confession, it seems, was it possible to open up and discuss a part of our history, i.e. the modernist rebuilding programme 1945-75, which had till then appeared, as Page put it, a 'Forbidden City'. Throughout the 1990s publications have also been issued (and sold well) by the RIAS and others, on such former modernist bogeymen as Basil Spence and Leslie Martin, and such buildings as St Peter's College, Cardross, which seems to indicate that a certain revaluation of work made taboo by the post-modern ethos is now taking place.

On a more popular note there has also been the success, throughout Scotland, of the Doors Open Day run, in Glasgow, by the Glasgow Buildings Preservation Trust. On one weekend per year (usually in September) the Trust arranges (in line with European Heritage Day) for the public to have the ability to enter free of charge and look around or be shown around 'some of the city's most exciting buildings'. The number of visitors increased from 18,000 recorded on the first Doors Open Day in 1990 to 98,000 in 1996. It is difficult, however, to say whether these figures reflect a real interest in architecture and buildings or just a measure of civic pride. Unfortunately, it has not been possible to obtain a breakdown of these figures in terms of what percentage visited old buildings and what new, or what was the social class and geographical origin of the visitors. These statistics would make for an interesting future study.

During the Year of Architecture and Design we might also learn something about the extent to which the attitude of 'people' versus 'architecture' can be changed, and how this antipathy affects the possibility of being a 'citizen' in Glasgow. Various initiatives have been set up by the Glasgow 1999 team which could act as go-between in this difficult area: first, there is the 1999 education programme which, with the help of a National Lottery award, aims to introduce young people and schoolchildren to concepts of architecture and design. The *Transformations on the Edge* programme aims at helping housing associations develop local run-down open spaces into significant parts of the cityscape (unfortunately this project has already suffered from lack of funding and has been scaled down and renamed *Millennium Spaces*). Then there is the Partnership Fund administered by 1999 to award money (£540,000 awarded) to community-based architecture or design-related projects. The question here though, is (following David Page's analysis) will it be enough, will these schemes have the wherewithal to take on, be properly informed by, and interact with, Glasgow's past? If not, what are they worth?

At any rate, for one year architecture in one form or other will take centre stage in the city's attempt at 'regeneration'. It remains to be seen how its official performance will measure up to that of 'The Garden' and 'Culture'. Meanwhile the reader of this guide will find listed here most new buildings that have appeared in central Glasgow over the last decade. You can read something about what has been built, how it has been built, who built it, and why. These architectural symptoms should help you make your own diagnosis as to whether the heart of Glasgow is expanding or contracting in 1999.

¹ **Glasgow Cathedral**

A competition to design an appropriate civic space around the medieval Cathedral was won in 1984 by Page & Park Architects. The brief called for the designers to give a sense of dignity to the space in front of the Cathedral, which had formerly been used as a car park for the Royal Infirmary; to provide 'framed' views of the traditional south-west aspect of the Cathedral (as in Thomas Hearne's painting of 1782, see *Central Glasgow*, p.11); and to break down the visual mass of the Royal Infirmary as seen up Castle Street. The winners responded with three projects:

Cathedral Visitors' Centre, 1991, Ian Begg with Page & Park Architects

A pastiche of Scots medieval complete with corbelled gable and turnpike stair, built with rubble cladding a reinforced concrete structure with wooden framed windows, and clearly meant to recreate the feel of the archbishop's palace (formerly on this site and finally destroyed in 1789). Ian Begg has completed other buildings elsewhere in this picturesque manner, including the former Scandic Hotel (now Holiday Inn Crowne Plaza) in Edinburgh and Raven's Craig in Plockton. Begg has said: 'I've tried to make statements, not of where we are, but restatements of roots and memory, and more than that, … of connecting points for people to see, and realise, this is Scotland.' Ironically this building has faced the same sort of 'Uncle Jock's carbuncle'-type criticism that was given to the original designs for the massive Royal Infirmary which overlooks it and dwarfs everything in the area. In 1901 they

thought 'Miller's baronial style inappropriate for a modern hospital' but by 1907 when building was underway it had been shorn of most of its baronial-type 'excrescences'. The Visitors' Centre now houses the **St Mungo Museum of Religious Art and History** and has within the walled enclosure to the rear a somewhat disappointing Japanese-style rock

15

garden. The framed views of the Cathedral and the Necropolis from both the large rear windows and the portico/cloister to the garden are splendid.

1 **Cathedral Court**, Milnbank Housing Association, 1991, Page & Park Architects
Built of Stanton Moor sandstone, split faced to give it a rubble effect, and with string-courses, tooled corners and ashlar margins, this housing echoes the three-storey mansion form of the Provand's Lordship but with a bulkier scale. Echoes of traditional detailing includes a steep slated roof with dormer windows, long overhanging eaves, gable ends, small individual windows to the rear and mullions on the larger windows to the front. Inside the 'amenities' include grab rails and non-slip floors. An internal courtyard looks out over the square, and

together with the St Mungo Museum this block forms the 'frame' for that south-west view of the Cathedral.

Glasgow Cathedral Precinct, 1991, Page & Park Architects in association with Ian White Landscape Architects
The square in front of the Cathedral is paved in stone and granite in a layout said by the architects to 'reflect and reinterpret the qualities of the nave of the Cathedral'. Trees have been planted forming a processional route towards the Cathedral, which help counter the dwarfing effect of the Royal Infirmary. The statue of David Livingstone has been placed in a prominent position at the front of the square facing Castle Street. Is there

significance in the fact that the 'Presbyterian saint' thus turns his back on Knox glowering down from the Necropolis?

2 **St Nicholas Garden**, 1996, James Cunning Young and Partners
This delightful green oasis behind Glasgow's oldest house (Provand's Lordship, 1471) with birds chirping and the sound of the traffic forgotten provides a pleasant contrast to the dismal barrenness of the so-called Japanese Garden behind the St Mungo Museum across the road. This contemporary reinterpretation of a medieval garden and cloister by architect Gary Johnson is the result of a competition held in 1993 by the

Right Aerial view of St Nicholas Garden with St Mungo's Museum and Cathedral in background (Anne Dick)

Glasgow Development Agency.

In horticultural terms the garden is laid out to represent the medieval/Renaissance intersection of the period when the house was built. Thus there is a contrast of cultivation for medicinal/culinary purposes and that for purely decorative ends. On the outer edge is the physic garden with plants which were used for medical purposes in the 15th century while in the centre is a knot based on a Celtic design. A camomile lawn is planted between the sett paving and when one walks over this, the stems are bruised and fragrance released.

The cloister runs along the west and north sides, has a panelled oak roof supported by oak purlins flitched with stainless steel, which rest in turn on the sandstone of the columns to the inner side, and the wall to the outer. Mounted at regular intervals along the west wall are the Tontine Heads, a series of grotesque carvings dated 1737 which formed the keystones of Alan Dreghorn's Tontine Building in Trongate (demolished 1869). These heads weigh one-third of a tonne each and the engineers, Buro Happold, 'devised a stainless-steel open-fronted box which is fixed into the reinforced-concrete beam of the stone-clad wall. On either side of each head, stainless-steel screws and padded plates act as clamps to hold the carving in place. Specially made pigmented resin bases support the heads on steel shelves.' The railings on the south side of the garden are by Jack Sloan, and the central grey granite carved font by Tim Pomeroy.

University of Strathclyde

The University of Strathclyde was awarded its charter in 1964 and from that time it began to expand in all directions from its original building, the Royal College of Science and Technology (see *Central Glasgow*, p.21) in George Street. Planning for this expansion has been controlled by various architects from RMJM to Walter Underwood and from GRM Kennedy to Gordon Cullen and, after a 1988 campus competition, has been in the hands of Page & Park. Each plan has left its traces but since Page & Park took over, the university has been gradually withdrawing all presence on Ingram Street and the south side of George Street to concentrate itself around what the architects call a 'processional route' along the hilltop ridge of Rottenrow and through the middle of the Royal College.

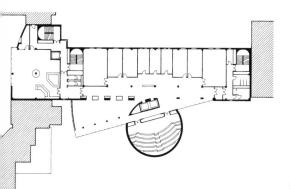

This route leads through the campus from St Paul's Chaplaincy to the Barony Church and thence to the Cathedral. It seems appropriate to nominate this a 'processional route' when one considers that Rottenrow is derived from the Gaelic *Rathad an righ* – the King's Road.

3 Graduate Business School, 1991, Reiach and Hall Architects

The architects here have used three simple geometric elements to effect (or perhaps to make manifest) a major transition in the university's role in, and attitude towards, the city. The original university buildings here from the late 1960s and 1970s present pretty drab brick façades and are orientated at an angle, turning away from Cathedral Street. The **Stenhouse** building (1972) for example, with its heavy cantilevered top

floor and tiny windows, has a monastic-cell-like quality and seems to turn away from the city, to say its business is private, ascetic. In the 1990s, however, the university is facing up to the city, looking for private finance, sponsorship etc., willing to welcome and to participate. How to bring the university back into the city? The three elements Reiach and Hall use in this building are, first, the spine. This building has a main brick-walled block which follows the angular orientation of the buildings around and thus declares itself part of the university. Second, there is the wedge, a glass-walled open-plan lounge area which juts out from the main spine and creates an urban frontage along Cathedral Street. The third element, the drum, is a red Corsehill sandstone-clad tower, which sits tangentially to the spine and has the wedge intersecting it as if to cut a section through it. On the ground floor the drum forms the entrance to the building and on the upper levels contains lecture theatres. While breaking up the dull modernist frontages, and restoring the urban and public element to the university, the angles that this monumental geometry presents to the street also serve to gather in and welcome the city to the rotunda entrance. Inside the open-plan wedge a variety of informal 'break out' spaces allow interaction in natural light along the axis of the street. The Bauhaus-style black-framed façade of the glass wall also provides an echo of the College of Building and Printing down the road (see *Central Glasgow*, p.22). Bedroom accommodation is provided on the top two

floors under the copper-clad roof (originally planned to be curved). Other interesting features are the curving brick wall to the garden side of the building which links the Stenhouse and William Duncan buildings, and has a geometrically appropriate extension of the spine – this time glazed like the wedge, and the bridge in glass and steel which curves over from the back of the building to the **William Duncan** building, demonstrating yet again how this work seeks to cohere, link and communicate.

3 **Institute of Health Sciences**, 1998,
Reiach and Hall Architects

Unlike the Graduate Business School, this building, faced on the north elevation in a similar red brick to that used on the spine of the Graduate Business School, does not make any attempt to realign the anti-urban

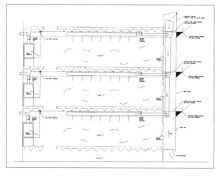

Opposite above Graduate Business School typical floor plan (level 3) (Reiach and Hall)
Opposite below 'The Drum' on Cathedral Street (Keith Hunter)
Above Institute of Health Sciences, section showing passive design of double glass wall (Reiach and Hall)
Below south elevation (Keith Hunter)

orientation of the existing university buildings, and sits well back off Cathedral Street, following the line of the Stenhouse building. It is not surprising to discover that this building houses labs for animal experiments – clearly the university is, despite all the rhetoric of the Graduate Business School, very choosy about the presentation of its 'public' face. This institute holds the departments of pharmaceutical science, physiology, pharmacology and immunology, and the official line is that the labs have to face southwards (that is to the private quiet seclusion of the university gardens, but, oddly, right in the glare of the sun) while the associated ancillary accommodation faces north (to the street and, of course, the shade) because of lab-area space requirements and the constraints of the surrounding buildings.

In this project Reiach and Hall have explored the potential for passive design. There is a double-skinned southerly glazed wall with the outer glazing layer sealed and the inner with opening windows. According to the architects, there are several advantages here: first, it is wide enough to provide walkways which can be used for window cleaning; these walkways then continue to the exterior and thus provide a deeper solar shading for the interior of the building. The outer glazed layer acts as a buffer against wind and rain, reducing unwanted infiltration and thus offering a greater potential for natural ventilation; it also provides a secure layer so that the inner glazing can be opened for night cooling. On warm sunny days the air in the void between the glazing layers will be warmed and a stack effect created which increases ventilation air movement. The louvres at the top of this void can be opened to release the hottest air. On cool but sunny days the louvres can be shut, and the heated air fed into the building's heating system.

It was estimated that the construction of this double façade added some £420,000 to the project cost, and simulation results (the architects worked with EDAS, Energy Design Advice Scheme) suggested fuel savings would make up the cost in ten years. One critic has said that 'such a long payback period would be unlikely to impress many speculative developers in the office sector'. But are these not the modes – innovative, experimental, risky business – in which the university ought to excel?

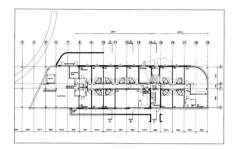

4 James Goold Hall, Rottenrow Student Residences, 1998, Page & Park Architects
Like the superstructure of some great ocean liner this building, with its curves and right angles and its cut-aways supported on pilotis, sails out from the brow of the brae of Rottenrow. A hybrid of the tenement and the slab block it wears its colours on its sleeve with the red brick clearly staking its claim for tenemental parentage and the white rendered planes and modernist glazing and metal cladding adding that high-flats style.

The architects intend some effect deeper than the skin here, however, trying to mesh the 'intimacy' of the tenement with the 'systemisation' of the slab block in order to reconcile the university development of the 1980s with its modernist expansion of the 1960s and 1970s.

5 St Andrew's Square, 1996, Robert Johnson Associates
One of the first 'Glasgow Squares' (see *Central Glasgow*, p.4), designed in 1786-8 by William Hamilton. The original was demolished in the 1980s. A new Black Pasture sandstone Georgian-style façade now reinstates the Glasgow square around St Andrew's Church (1739, undergoing refurbishment as a centre of traditional music and dance to be completed by 2000).

The design of the frontage was developed according to the architect, 'in response to the character and scale of the Georgian (*sic*) church'. Above the four storeys of sandstone frontage is a recessed rendered attic floor behind a continuous balcony. The problem here is that there appear to be too many floors, given the height of the façade, to gain a real Georgian effect; thus the windows have a small, cramped appearance rather than grand and elegant. The rear

elevations have post-modern housing details, bands of coloured brick, stylised pediments, pagoda roofs, finials railings and balconies overlooking the green.

6 **Homes for the Future**

This development on a 1.5 acre brownfield site between St Andrew's Square and Glasgow Green is said by the Glasgow 1999 team to be one of their 'flagship' projects which will show 'how Glasgow can take the lead in regenerating its inner-city housing areas and its economic base'. The master planners for the site were Page & Park Architects with Arup Associates and the aim is to re-establish the urban fabric of an old part of central Glasgow by planning for specific types of building, i.e. 'grand urban apartments', 'terraced apartments', 'town

houses', 'garden houses' and 'landmark buildings', to be sited in accordance with a strict formalisation of the relationship between the Green and the city streets.

This project was put together very quickly. A competition was then held for the individual sites within the plan, and by July 1999 the first part of the development will be completed and opened to the public as the Glasgow 99 Expo. At the launch of this Glasgow 1999 project (in London, curiously), David Page seemed to be anticipating some particular criticism when he stressed that this is 'not an architectural zoo'. He could not thus have been totally surprised when Isi Metzstein, former professor at Edinburgh University and designer of the only existing building on the site (Our Lady and St Francis School), wrote of the non-grid-iron site (*Architects' Journal*, Jan. 1999) that it '… does not suggest opportunities for prototypical demonstration relevant to Glasgow's grammar of built form', and, of the plans, that he found '… the apparent inability of the zoo of projects to relate to the existing building, never mind to each other, both ominous and sad.'

The schemes already under way are by:

Elder and Cannon Architects

The first of the 'grand apartments' addressing the Green. A seven-storey steel-frame building with a glass lift, extensive glazing and balconies to the south for solar effects and views over the park.

Rick Mather

Another 'grand apartment' block, all the units here have views in two directions to capture any available sunshine during the day.

Ushida Findlay

The hexagonal geometric form of this building has an 'object quality' and forms a tower to the Green, with terraces stepping down progressively and leading back up Lanark Lane. A pend through the building leads to the communal gardens and allows complete circulation 'around' the object. The curved geometric motifs here are typical of this Tokyo firm's work, but this is their first project in this country. Findlay is originally from Cupar, but one has to wonder if she has forgotten about the weather here – north-facing terraces in Glasgow?

McKeown Alexander Architects

A four-storey tower with large glazed screen 'acts as a punctuation mark' on the northernmost site, while down the western edge adjacent to St Andrew's Square is a terrace of 'town houses'.

Above Ushida Findlay block, south elevation to Green (Glasgow 1999)
Below Ushida Findlay block, north elevation (Glasgow 1999)

Ian Ritchie Architects

Ian Ritchie won Thenew Housing Association's competition for this last 'grand apartment' block to be sited next to Gillespie Kidd & Coia's A-listed Our Lady and St

Francis school of 1964 (see *Central Glasgow*, p.35). Two steel-framed oblong towers with full glazed windows overlooking the park and joined in the middle by a stair tower/elevator shaft, will provide association houses for rent.

Wren Rutherford ASL

Two houses on the first, very narrow site (7.5m) on Lanark Street. One large house and one small, they are stacked on top of one another with a southerly hard-paved courtyard which can be closed off with sliding screens. Each house is accessed through south-facing conservatories. There should be no problem selling these as Mactaggart & Mickel (the developers) claim a world record in number of houses sold in 24 hours.

RMJM Scotland Ltd

A small block of four flats and two maisonettes sit one above the other in a

rendered tower both with access to a roof garden. Three timber-clad flats sit above a ground-floor flat which is rendered to match the tower.

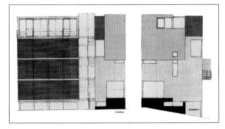

Left above Computer-generated image of McKeown Alexander's terrace and tower (McKeown Alexander)
Left below Ian Ritchie Architects' block (Glasgow 1999)
Right above One of RMJM's blocks (RMJM)
Right below Wren Rutherford's houses (Wren Rutherford)

7 Saltmarket Housing, 1994,
Nicholas Groves-Raines

Housing development for GAP Housing Association as an infill for an urban block once bounded on all sides by Victorian tenements but of which only one corner remained. As an experiment in exposing the traditional tenement block to openness, light and geometric playfulness it is largely successful. The Saltmarket frontage restores the urban corridor, while the crescent-shaped terrace on the opposite corner with its canopies, turret-like forms and raised parapets give both a southerly view over the park and an elegant post-modern flourish towards the baroque detailing of St Andrew's-in-the-Green Church.

Less successful is the **ARC** by Gerry Connolly whose quarter circle of brick housing on a deck-access balcony raised above garages has none of the light touch and playfulness of its neighbour, and simply leans oppressively round the church.

8 Justiciary Court Extension, Jocelyn Square, 1997, TPS Consultants

The portico of William Stark's original High Court Building (1809) facing onto the Green across Saltmarket was said to have the first strictly correct Doric proportions (in accordance with those of Theseion of Athens) in Scotland, and this extension to the building squeezed into a tight site between Paddy's Market and a Salvation Army building on Clyde Street won't let us forget it. Right at the entrance to the new extension we have the first play on the theme – a tempietto-type Doric circular portico with sandstone columns mounted on granite plinths. Beyond this is the golden flower marble-floored and travertine-walled atrium lit by the glass curtain east-facing wall. Here again we are struck by the rhythm of two-storey columns, supporting the

Above Justiciary Court Extension (Keith Hunter)

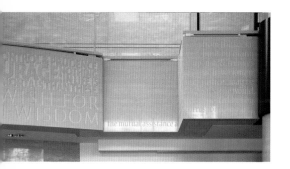

balcony round three sides of the atrium. This balcony holds what might be said to be the strongest feature: the carved Portuguese limestone frieze by artist Gary Breeze.

Breeze has carved overlapping excerpts from three different texts in different styles: from Hume's *Commentary on the Law of Scotland* (representing The Law, in roman type), from Hume's *Enquiries Concerning the Principles of Morals* (representing the Word of Man in cursive hand-written style), and from the *Book of Solomon* (representing the Word of God, grit blasted in bold capitals). It is difficult to say whether this frieze should inspire or disturb the visitor – it probably depends on the nature of the appointment. At any rate the cliché 'set in stone' is more than obvious, but either way the frieze can no more be passed over lightly than can the business of the court.

Inside there are six new courtrooms where the classical theme is continued with pearwood wall panelling, and natural light is drawn through roof glazing integrated into the coffered ceilings. Limited to the height of the existing High Court it is built with a steel-frame roof structure over a reinforced-concrete frame on pile foundations. At the intersection between the two parts of the building, old and new, is a tiny Tivoli-type water garden designed as a contemplative space; unfortunately it is here that – perhaps in an attempt to humanise the strict orders – the rhythm of the much more diminutive Doric peristyle in Crossland Hill sandstone is somewhat agley from the rest of the building. To be fair, this effect might be lessened when the plantings around this feature begin to develop.

8 **Jocelyn Square Housing**, Mart Street/ St Margaret's Place, completion 2000, Kinnear & Crotch

This project illustrates both the pros and cons for the design process when progressive young architects take the initiative to generate work for themselves in Glasgow. These architects, who have connections with both Strathclyde University and the Mackintosh School of Architecture, sought

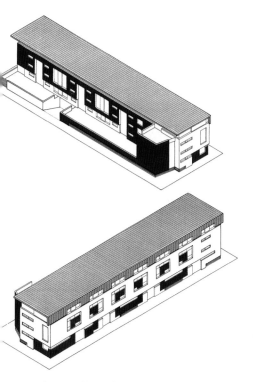

development here. The site is unpromising, only 15m deep, would have restrictions placed on window size and placement for privacy's sake (due to the proximity of residential housing on the other side of St Margaret's Place), and had already suffered two planning permission rejections in 1991 and 1993 by other architects.

The narrowness of the site precludes possibility of the traditional 'doughnut'-style block with a middle courtyard, and this already points to a difficulty with the creation of the requisite number of car-parking spaces. Kinnear & Crotch decided to opt for a 'coffin block', a long narrow construction which is given extra solidity and monumentality by being contained within the folded-over zinc standing-seam roof. The problem with the St Margaret's

Place windows is solved by creating bedrooms only to that side of the building, which need only narrow shoulder height windows in the façade.

These windows are then recessed behind a flowing composition of two different coloured façades which, as planes of different depths, interpenetrate one another and create a strange weightless unsupported effect while still reproducing something like the traditional tenement solid/void (i.e. window/stone face) ratio. The car-parking problem is solved by shifting it underground into the basement of the original tenement on this site, and the corner feature extending along Jocelyn Square towards the new Justiciary Court helps to border what the architects hope can become a new public space.

out this site themselves and set about convincing planners and developers of the possibilities and indeed necessity of

Above & below Jocelyn Square project (Kinnear & Crotch Architects)

9 **Carrick Quay**, Clyde Street, 1989,
Davis Duncan Partnership
Modernist block named after, and designed
to look out over the clipper, the *Carrick*,
which was berthed in the Clyde below.
The architects here sought not only to
repair a major urban block on the periphery
of the city centre, but to mediate between
the disparate architectural influences
(massive stone river-front warehouses, red
city-improvement tenements, the Gothic
Merchant's Steeple, the moored ship itself,
and the white-painted French classical
façade of the Briggait Centre) which bear
upon this area.

Thus the red-and-buff brickwork wall is
surmounted by a lightweight steel system of
balconies, terraces, railings and gangways
which lend the mass of the façade a certain
verticality and nautical flavour. Misfortune
overtook this project in the form of the
economic recession of the early 1990s, and
also, ironically, in the removal of the *Carrick*
from its berth on the river. Many of the flats
were empty with For Sale signs stuck outside
for years, and the site of Phase 2, round into
Stockwell Street, lay as a vacant lot
throughout the period. English post-
modernist architect Piers Gough has
commented that the real cause of its
languishing incomplete throughout those
years was, in his opinion, because the steel
system of balconies and terraces had been
painted black instead of white. Davis

Duncan, however, are unrepentant; they
claim for the project a 'rigorous adherence
to basic tenets of the modern movement'
and that it is 'totally independent from the
vagaries of stylistic whim'.

River Clyde
Since the Clyde's days as a working river
came to an end there have been many
projects to revitalise it, to attempt to
transform it from an industrial ruin and find
some new role for it in the city. Some of
these schemes have been private piecemeal
or small-scale; like the housing at
Lancefield Quay and on the other bank on
either side of the **Kingston Bridge**, the
Quay leisure and entertainment
development in **Springfield Quay**, the
conservation work on **Carlton Place**, and

the walkways constructed along the north bank from where the quayside warehouses were removed. There was even a waterbus along the river during 1990. On the other hand, there have also been some more comprehensive development initiatives. A plan to convert the Queen's Dock into a maritime museum seems to have run out of steam, while the **Scottish National Science Centre** in the Pacific Quay (see p.36) is going ahead. In 1996, stimulated by the imminent, as it seemed then, demolition of the Meadowside Granary, the Glasgow Institute of Architects held a weekend-long, convention/workshop called 'Bringing the City to the River' attended by people from many fields. The ideas and projects discussed there were then published in a book by Park Circus Promotions. The latest strategic plan

for the Clyde, by consultant architects Zogolovitch and Alsop acting for the City Planning Department, is to build a weir over the Clyde at the mouth of the River Kelvin. The architects themselves say this is still an 'idea not a reality' and that it would need a substantial investment of public money. In *Macjournal 3* (1998), published by Mackintosh School of Architecture, architects McKeown Alexander edited the work of 14 Glasgow architects' elaborations on this strategic plan, called 'River of Dreams'.

In the space between the railway bridge and the Glasgow road bridge (or Jamaica Bridge, original by Telford) Victorian engineers, Blyth & Cunningham, constructed two sets of Dalbeattie granite piers for an anticipated expansion in rail

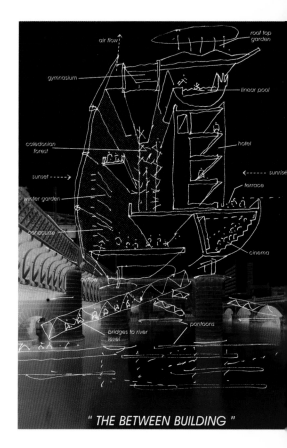

" THE BETWEEN BUILDING "

10

Above The Between Building (Andrew Lee-photography, McKeown Alexander-sketch)

transportation. McKeown Alexander see a possibility for expansion as coming to fruition with the Channel rail link to continental Europe. These piers were carved with an inscription 'All greatness stands firm in the storm' in both original Greek and English translation by the artist Ian Hamilton Finlay in 1990. The English translation is a rewording, after Heidegger, of a line from the sixth book of Plato's *Republic*. It has been suggested that a more accurate translation of the Greek would be 'all great things are precarious'. Perhaps that would have been a better motto for the Clyde.

11 **Riverboat Casino**, Broomielaw, 1996, Crerar & Partners

A box pavilion clad in grey granite on black marble base with some textbook 1930s-style details. Steel-framed with four reinforced-concrete stair towers, a fully glazed *piano nobile* first floor, it has an oversailing aluminium sheet butterfly roof and a balcony with nautical-style railings facing over the Clyde. 'Night architecture' – the coloured strip neon and the bright red sign are presumably meant to act as a beacon, calling gamblers over from the south side. On the Broomielaw elevation the sailing/riverboat metaphor is continued with oversailing roof, a neon-lighted mast, and a series of fins running vertically up the façade. During substructure excavations china deposits were found and identified as ceramics from the Britannia and Verreville potteries, giving credence to theories of 19th-century pottery production in Glasgow.

11 **Atlantic Quay**, Broomielaw, phase one, 1990, Building Design Partnership

The largest single commercial development in Scotland, this first phase sites three buildings around a central piazza between Robertson Street and York Street and soon a fourth will be added to complete the composition. This historic tobacco-warehouse district was derelict and the intention is to 'reinforce the river edge by providing a coherent and continuous front onto the Clyde linking the city with the river'.

No 1 Atlantic Quay on the corner of Robertson Street and the Broomielaw is a forceful anodised aluminium-clad block with external full-height columns holding up floors four and five above the deeply recessed floors below to create a sweeping loggia form which rounds the corner. The building thus echoes the turn, the cornice height and the rhythm of the pilasters on the Clyde Port Authority (see *Central Glasgow*, pp.44-5), and its crisp modernist geometry needs no excuses beside the complex elevations of the older building.

31

The other two buildings are clad in salmon-pink granite with minimal aluminium features – on the corner of York Street a small cupola echoes that on the Port Authority. Between the two buildings onto the Broomielaw is a landscaped stepped lane up to the central piazza which is tucked in behind the buildings and of which the architects say it is 'first in a series of new civic spaces'. Is this just planners' talk? In what sense are these words, 'first', 'civic' and 'space' used here when it would appear doubtful if anyone will ever use this left-over area in any role other than as an employee of the tenants? A more honest and realistic part of the development as regards the 'users' is the underground parking below this piazza which is accessed by a ramp between the buildings on Robertson Street.

12 **BT Broomielaw**, 1999, Fitzroy Robinson
Six-storey steel-framed building with the largest atrium (33m by 33m in a building 66m wide) in Scotland, for which a special relaxation of Technical Standards was obtained in order to leave it open, unglazed, on floors one, two and three.

The entrance to the building is to the rear, north side, between metal and glass-clad towers. From the piazza the Kirkstone slabbing continues to the interior and one is immediately struck by the vastness and light of the space. Despite the south-facing façade there is minimum glare and the main office space is 15m column-free (achieved by cell-form beams).

The towers, the glass curtain walling (somewhat reminiscent of the County

Buildings in Hamilton), the soaring glass elevators on the atrium walls, and metal oversailing roof with swelling support piers keep up the high-tech front along the new riverside, and seem specially appropriate given this building's situation on *James Watt Street*. Unfortunately, the massing on the Broomielaw façade, although clad in aluminium, is quite unsubtle, especially compared to the Robertson Street corner.

Can development of the site immediately west make this good?

Atlantic Square, completion 2000, Building Design Partnership
To the north of the BT building BDP continue their redevelopment of this area with plans for 'hotel, retail and restaurant activity' as well as a new office tower curved in plan which will be a 'significant landmark building'. This starts to sound a bit more like a 'civic space'.

13 Lancefield Quay Housing, 1990, Thomson McCrea & Sanders
Clyde Navigation Trust sheds, originally built in 1948 and used for storing grain, were here converted to 92 houses. Owing to poor ground conditions on the quay the loadings of this development are transferred to the original frame and piles. The top section of the sheds were removed and the original first-floor slab used as a base for the new timber-frame housing. A mezzanine floor is suspended from this base and two new floors built on top. It is just as well that 112 covered parking spaces are provided inside the complex because if the residents had to go for a pint of milk by foot it might take them a while. This part of the river front is pretty isolated, cut off from the city by industrial areas. On the riverside elevation every flat has a terrace, and the step-back means that the development maintains, appropriately enough for a Wimpey project, a quite suburban feel to it. On the roadside/north elevation there is a more tenemental scale with a nautical post-modern flavour – original sandstone pediments, roundel air ducts, dormer windows and glass-fronted stairwells with pitched roofs. On a picturesque note, it is from this quay that the *Waverley* – the only remaining sea-going paddle-steamer in the world – sails.

Above Section of Lancefield Quay Housing (Thomson McCrea Architects)

14 **Clyde Auditorium**, 1997,
Norman Foster and Partners

The brief for this project was to create a building more distinctive than the existing sheds that made up the SECC complex, which offered the facility to drive trucks directly onto its stage (complete with fly-tower, wings and full backstage facilities) while also providing direct links to extensive exhibition spaces, along with electronic delegate voting systems, simultaneous translation, projection and sound-control booths. Foster and Partners' contention is that the exterior form of the building evolved from the internal planning (over 4000 drawings were produced for the steelwork package alone), which wraps accommodation in a series of layers around the auditorium. However this form was attained, the simple fact is that the Clyde Auditorium with its roofscape of eight overlapping aluminium-clad shells has become not just a functional building, but an object in itself, an instant and distinctive

landmark in the city, while from within the building the glazed foyer spaces between those shells allow views back up the river

towards Glasgow. The auditorium itself is capable of seating 3029 on three tiered levels, which makes it one-quarter again the size of the Royal Concert Hall and places it amongst the top four conference venues in Europe.

While some have claimed to see a zoomorphic element in its unusual curved shape – it is already widely known to the Glasgow public as the 'Armadillo' – and others still see similarities to the Sydney Opera House, it seems clear after a moment's reflection that the building's roof form, sitting here as it does, by the River Clyde, makes some gesture towards the shipping tradition of this city. It has been suggested these vast shells are like sections of ships' hulls, but it could even be said that the way the shells overlap recalls the clinkerbuilt construction technique and, in fact, to stand in the foyer under the soaring roof with all the steel and concrete structure exposed is like nothing more than sheltering under a vast upturned rowing boat. It might be interesting to know whether Foster, in his designing of a conference centre, knew of the Gaelic Bardic tradition where the poet would lie under an upturned boat to meditate on his verse, but what seems, for the moment, of a much wider and more pressing importance is the whole issue of metaphor in Scottish architecture. Why is it that architects from beyond Glasgow and Scotland appear to be so ready to adopt shipping and navigational metaphor in their built work in this country (see for example

Opposite Clyde Auditorium (left) & No.1 Pacific Quay (right) (Keith Hunter)
Left Structural detail of Clyde Auditorium (Keith Hunter)
Above Section of Clyde Auditorium (Norman Foster and Partners)

CZWG's Wheatley and Cotton Houses (p.49); Branson Coats' Bargo (p.48) and of course Enric Miralles' design based on upturned fishing boats for the Scottish Parliament) when our home-based architects show little inclination to adopt this type of design?

15 Pacific Quay

The masterplan for the development of this 75-acre site with 2km of waterfront was

prepared by the Parr Partnership. The development will include a hotel, the new BBC Scotland headquarters, Scottish National Science Centre and a business park fronting along the Clyde, of which phase one (One Pacific Quay) has already been completed.

One Pacific Quay, 1998,
The Parr Partnership

This elegant three-storey building with one wing sitting along parallel to the river and the other at the perpendicular contributes to the high-tech feel of the riverside, with the Clyde Auditorium and the Moat Hotel on the other side of Bell's Bridge. Each floor is fully glazed with only the service core, wing towers and the oversailing roof/aerofoil being metal clad. Part of the development was to convert the Four Winds Pavilion in

red sandstone with a heavy Florentine Renaissance tower. The scheme, to a certain extent, has rescued the Pavilion from the desolation in which it languished unseen, restoring it to a built environment, but the problem seems to be that the buildings are jammed up too close together, a fact which detracts from that aforementioned elegance.

15 Scottish National Science Centre, completion date 2000, Building Design Partnership

To be built on the site of the Garden Festival, the Centre comprises a 10,500 m^2 Exploratorium, a 350-seat Imax theatre and a 100m-high tower. The form of the Exploratorium is a glazed pod which wraps around a deck with a series of exhibition boxes or containers – 'like peas in a pod' – as the architects say. A neat complement to

Above Clydeway Skypark (1969 Jack Holmes & Partners), reclad in aluminium rain-screen and glass curtain walling by Bonar Grams Architects (1998). It now makes up the third silvered vertex (Armadillo-Pacific Quay-Skypark) of a topographical triangle (Gerry Grams)
Opposite CAD images of proposed Scottish National Science Centre (Building Design Partnership)

the 'Armadillo' on the other bank, one wonders what witty moniker this erection might earn for itself. The tower designed by Richard Horden originally won the competition to be sited at St Enoch's Square. Designed as a vertical wing to turn into the wind and reduce drag, it will be built of aluminium and lightweight steel, and turn on oil-film bearings. By turning the structure into the wind, the architects say 30% of weight and material can be saved compared to a conventional structure.

16 **Tron Theatre Redevelopment**,
Chisholm Street, 1998, RMJM (formerly
Tron steeple, 1586; Tron Kirk, 1793-5,
J Adam, screen wall, 1899, J J Burnet)

Unity in continuity in both material and
form seems to be the theme of architects
Paul Stallon and Alan Dickson's sensitive
redevelopment of this guddle of buildings of
various ages and styles. They refer to the
complex centred on Adam's plain church as
a 'city in miniature', and the church itself as
a jewel held in the city block's interior. The
first phase exploits a technical solution to
poetic effect on that theme: a three-storey
glass-walled atrium is placed *crystal-like*
behind the steeple and the Burnet screen
wall. As a box office, this space with its cool
colours, geometry and materials (black slate,
timber, white render and red booking desk)
and its view of the solid bulk of Adam's

church pressing, it
almost seems, up against
the glass, already creates
a feeling of high drama.

With phase two, the
frontage of new offices
and bar along Chisholm
Street and round into
Parnie Street continue
the effect of Burnet's
screen wall. It is here
with that façade we
really see the attention
that has been paid to
detail in order to achieve
that unity in continuity
of materials and forms.
Now the jewel is fully
clasped, with the

Right Tron Theatre Box Office (Keith Hunter)

38

three-storey modern sandstone cladding flaunting its superficiality and its simple non-load-bearing function while Burnet's baroque presents a near-solid front to the street. The new wall has multiple punched-through openings, doors and windows into the offices and bars, and also a large double-height window turning the corner, where the Burnet wall gives only smaller geometric clues to its real function.

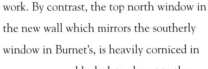

The aluminium framing around the main windows gives a rhythmic echo of the balustrades of the older wall, while holding in place the timber slats which provide a light tricky balance to the mass of Burnet's work. By contrast, the top north window in the new wall which mirrors the southerly window in Burnet's, is heavily corniced in black slate almost to the point of being an open cubist turret, thus jutting its chin out cheekily towards Rochead's baronial extravaganza in Trongate (see *Central Glasgow*, p.58).

The downsides of this development are the aluminium *brise-soleil* above both the box office and the bar/offices – they seem somehow flimsy and set at odd angles – and the camp cabbage-patch-type golden cherub placed in the niche on Burnet's wall just below the steeple – it represents nothing but a puerile gesture towards the whole idea of historicity, unity and continuity. A pity given the architect's sensitive reworking of the block. There is a right place for kitsch, no doubt, and especially so, one imagines, in a post-industrial city, but is it then too pompous to ask if the Florentines would have the urge to stick some tacky-looking gewgaw in a niche below the third oldest structure in their city?

The third phase, the redevelopment of the auditorium itself, will be completed in 1999.

Merchant City

This area north of Trongate and east of Buchanan Street was named 'Merchant City' by Charles McKean in a 1971 analysis in *Architectural Design*. From 1980 there was large-scale investment here, as part of the SDA's City Centre project, and within the

39

decade 1143 houses had been built or converted in the area. As Glendinning *et al* said of it in *History of Scottish Architecture*: 'The guiding philosophy was that of accentuating the "mixed" character by a combination of new building and rehabilitation, pushing it upmarket by introducing groups of higher-income dwellings.'

It is this latter feature that seems to have focused criticism of the project. Some might even say that the whole post-modern project has only served to complete the modernist programme of removing the workers and lower classes from the city centre to outlying schemes, by then sanitising the post-industrial ruins for the middle class. Is that in any way an accurate view? Certainly there has not only been disagreement about the politics of this regeneration, but even dissent

over the possibility of calling this area the 'Merchant City'.

One pressure group, which campaigned against what it saw as the packaging and hype of such regeneration, which organised demonstrations and produced a satirical news-sheet called *The Keelie*, chose its name 'Workers' City' specifically to oppose the notion of the 'Merchants' City'. One of the members of this group, the writer James Kelman, said this name was picked to highlight 'the grossness of the fallacy that Glasgow somehow exists because of the tireless efforts of a tiny patriotic coalition of fearless 18th-century entrepreneurs and far-sighted politicians. These same merchants and politicians made the bulk of their personal fortunes by the simple expedient of not paying for the price of labour.'

Despite such opposition, it appears that now the name 'Merchant City' has established itself, perhaps because the only real alternative, its original name as the 'New Town', is nowadays too closely associated with post-war developments such as East Kilbride or Cumbernauld.

17 **The Italian Centre**, John Street, 1991, Page & Park Architects

This scheme, which converted a series of semi-derelict listed warehouse buildings fronting onto three streets into a complex of retail units, restaurants, cafés, flats and offices, is often cited as *the* success of the Merchant City. By selective removal of buildings in the rear to form a large courtyard, the architects were able to base this project on the form of an Italian palazzo, 'where external elevational restraint is set against the visual excitement and vibrancy of the courtyard'.

Inside the courtyard the Italian feel is strengthened by the openness to the street – four pends lead into the court – the double-fronted shop and café units onto the courtyard as well as the street, the covered inner walkway in Bologna-portico style alongside those retail units, the pastel shade of rendering used on the walls and, of course, the integrated craft and art works. (Ten per cent of the development costs were spent on art and craft works.)

The sculpture and frieze work on the north elevation of the courtyard by Jack Sloan joins with the balconies and sunshades into one bristling metalwork frontage. The frieze is an Italian futurist-style

representation of Phaeton's journey with Apollo's sun-chariot, drawn out across metal Persian shutters which are mounted on rails across the top-floor windows. On the ground in the courtyard itself is the quirky *Man-and-Dog* representation by Shona Kinloch. The fountain and long channel of flowing water with the banded stonework on the ground floor behind is reminiscent of the works of Italian master Carlo Scarpa.

The external façades of the buildings are kept austerely classical, with heavy cornicing and an additional monumentality created by the sculpture of Sandy Stoddart. On the elevation to John Street, and down in the street itself (now pedestrianised and very busy with pavement cafés) are his three representations of *Mercury* (Mercury, Mercurial, Mercurius), a study in the brass-

necked deity's place and influence in the activity of this 'Merchant City'. Above the elevation to Stockwell Street is *Italia*, a standing berobed female.

17 178-180 Ingram Street, 1994, Page & Park Architects
This Mannerist, sandstone-clad infill replaces a building destroyed by fire next door to the main Italian Centre. Visually arresting are

41

Above 178-180 Ingram Street (Anne Dick)

the heavy patinated phosphor-bronze shutters decorated with whirling vortex patterns based on a thistle motif. Once the passer-by has stopped to gaze at these, the other more subtle sculptural details of the other two floors gradually manifest themselves. On the middle floor the heavy bronze window surrounds are decorated with fasces, and on the ground floor the piers which separate the bays of the shop front have been transformed into pilasters by the simple placing at the summit of small green bronze capitals of different orders. These capitals encase the sculpted heads of men identified with the early development of the Merchant City. At the base of the piers is a plaque inscribed with the appropriate name, business and dates of the individuals represented.

Ultimately it must be said that the façade is tricked out in such an armoury of sculpture that one wonders what or who it is trying to scare off – the *architectural* critic perhaps?

18 **107 Ingram Street**, 1989,
Elder and Cannon Architects
Infill four-storey block of flats between a Victorian warehouse in Scottish baronial and Dutch details (now converted to housing) and a 1930s-style corner office block. It seemed to the architects then that there was no point trying to blend this building with its neighbours and it was given 'its own personality'. The colour was suggested by the north-facing orientation of the façade. The black glazed bricks are built with 6mm joints to maximise the qualities of the shiny surface

and the details are kept simple to emphasise this characteristic. Bands of blue glazed bricks do, however, draw the eyes up to the top floor where, over the centre bay, a cubist-type feature encloses the French windows in an echo of the Dutch gables and baronial turrets of next door.

19 **Brunswick Hotel**, 106-108 Brunswick Street, 1996, Elder and Cannon Architects
As part of their Ingram Square development this site presented the problem of stepping across the narrow gap from a five-storey French Renaissance building to a crazy three-storey baronial invention (see *Central Glasgow*, p.72). On the other hand, it might be said that the variety of massing and scale in this street left the architects with a free hand. The result is an elegant eight-storey hotel which is divided vertically into three

separate zones each articulated through different materials and form.

The ground floor has a continuously glazed frontage which opens onto the reception and café bar (fitted out colourfully in a mix of hard and soft furnishings by Graven Images) and restaurant in the basement.

Above the canopy are four stone-faced classically austere floors with flush rows of windows following the horizontal pattern of the street.

Left Brunswick Hotel (Keith Hunter)
Above Basement Bar (Keith Hunter)

The upper two floors, the penthouse suite as a double-height unit, offcentre – or deconstruct – this classical geometry with an oversailing roof pointing a finger, as if in fun, over at the diminutive pediment next door at No 114 and beyond to the baronial madness of Nos 118-128 while a stepped cornice both separates the penthouse from those floors below and helps the step down between its neighbours on either side. The roof walls and soffit of this penthouse are covered in long-strip copper with standing seams, in a design which is rather too heavy and owes a lot to the detailing of the much-copied Münster Library in Germany by architects Bolles Wilson.

20 City Halls, Fruitmarket Block,
Candleriggs/Bell Street/Albion Street

After the original burst of redevelopment in the 1980s much of the Merchant City languished in its original dilapidated state through the early 1990s. Many explanations have been put forward; it is said that the City Council ran out of properties it owned, which it had bought up in the doldrum years of the 1950s and 1960s (e.g. the buildings of The Italian Centre) and had used to stimulate development; the simple fact of the economic recession is also blamed, but at any rate the whole project of 'Merchant Citifying' the area had a half-hearted air about it. In the late 1990s this began to change, however, and this city block typifies the onward march of 'regeneration'. The former Fruitmarket, subsequently the Candleriggs market, is being transformed by large commercial developers into a complex of restaurants, bars and cafés around a

central courtyard, and the basement area is to be converted to a nightclub. There has been some concern about the effects of these 'super pubs' and 'theme bars' on local trade, but there have also been a couple of interesting developments on this block:

Ticket Centre, Candleriggs, 1995, McInnes Gardner

If Glasgow's attempt to create a 'new image' as a 'city of culture' is to be taken seriously then its main ticket outlet must be something other than 'shabby', 'anonymous', 'cramped' and 'down at heel' (description of the former building on George Square by the architects). Their new design is smart and clean cut on the outside; a plain black frontage with stainless-steel lettering of minimum elevation; but once inside everything is wittily surreal with luvvy-type metaphors of the world of performance. Four curving counters with swelling black piers ('ballerina's legs') give the feel of giant piano ebonies, while the red profiled cladding below is a reference to stage curtains. The display space with its drum and domed ceiling, sound hole black floor and system of suspension wires and fastenings also leaves nothing much to be said. Have they over-egged the custard pie? No, it's just good fun.

Interval Bar, City Halls, Candleriggs, 1998, Zoo Architects

City Halls façade has been cleaned, new artwork been set in the pavement, and now the disused toilets to the north of the main entrance have been converted into an interval bar. (A metaphor for Glasgow? For its cultural interregnum?) A barrel-vaulted room with cast-iron supports and a sandstone gable wall this space has to cater efficiently for 300-400 people at theatre intervals. Thus the bar is unfurnished with a

Opposite above En-suite bathroom (Andrew Lee) *Opposite below* Penthouse suite (Keith Hunter)
Left Candleriggs Market, Bell Street elevation (Gilchrist Briggs)

simple 10m-long rigidified metal bar down one side and a shelf along the other where the original fenestration on the cast-iron façade has been restored. Uplighting of the vault and coloured floor lights which fill holes left by the old WC soil pipes create the required low-key ambience.

21 **Todd Building** (original 1899, Henry Clifford), Ingram Street/Albion Street, redevelopment & new-build, 1997-9, James Cunning Young & Partners

This project to bring loft apartments to Glasgow has two phases: the conversion of the Todd, a six-storey redstone building (originally a clothing factory but latterly belonging to the University of Strathclyde when it was used among other things for experimenting with the effects of lead poisoning on rats) and the construction of a totally new building adjacent to the old one.

Three lofts have already been fitted out in the original building, one by Graven Images, one by Zoo Architects and another by Gareth Hoskins Architects.

The new steel-framed building is a typical modernist composition, reminiscent of the work of Italian modernist Giuseppe Terragni, with a black granite plinth surmounted by a white cuboid which is cut open with long glass-wall frontages on two sides, both to reveal the inner volume and to expose the interior to light. The curved oversailing roof seems to be forced up spontaneously Jack-in-the-box style by the volume of the penthouse thrusting up out the main body of the building.

How would the modernist masters feel to hear themselves cited in the trendy wars? In their brochure the developers do not hesitate to exploit the rhetoric: 'The Bauhaus and villas of Le Corbusier still exemplify this progressive spirit; living spaces liberated from fixed walls and rigid rooms; apartments and houses defined by volume and area and not just by room count.' After such dubious and crass claims

Above Interval Bar (Andrew Lee)
Opposite left Interior of Todd Building flat by Zoo Architects (Andrew Lee)
Opposite right Multi-storey car park, Candleriggs elevation (Anne Dick)

46

for an architectural genealogy the really progressive question remains – can one liberate *any* space while simultaneously depoliticising it? Or – is the desert a space?

22 Multi-storey car park,
Candleriggs/Albion Street, 1990,
The Carl Fisher Sibbald Partnership
This reinforced-concrete structure, clad externally in brickwork with bush-hammered painted concrete string-courses and decorative metal panels, is the car park as art deco folly. Spanning the whole city block, on the pedestrian side, to Candleriggs, it masquerades as a 'normal' building with shopfronts along at ground level, soaring canted bays with black metal railings, a split pediment above the middle bay, tall stone pilasters and fake dormer windows, all of which echo the details of surrounding buildings – especially the classical red sandstone into Bell Street. On Albion Street, however, the elevation is more banal and utilitarian with the glaring signposts and gaping entry ways of the standard car park. Structure is a portal frame design, spanning 52 ft without internal columns or stiffening walls – thus more space for the driver to manoeuvre.

23 **Greyfriars Court**, 88 Albion Street, 1998, Cooper Cromar

U-shaped block of housing taking in Albion Street, Blackfriars Street and Wall Street. The 1930s modern-style tower on the Albion/Blackfriars corner balances the block as bookend with the large classical building on the Bell Street corner. In between those, the use of red brick and white render on the top floor is an attempt to relate the façade to the scale of the low red sandstone Cheesemarket – now Bargo. Entrance by glazed pend from Albion Street leads up a stairway to a raised courtyard with four corner stair towers.

23 **Bargo**, Albion Street, 1996, Branson Coates

This bar with a chirpy industrial atmosphere exploits the deceptively high space in the interior of the former cheesemarket building. The massive mezzanine landing keeps the chunky scale round the walls from behind a floor-to-ceiling tall curved open screen of timbers. A suspended and illuminated mesh canopy can have its height adjusted to emphasise the volume. The furniture on the other hand is quite dinky: zinc-topped tables and beech stools with silver vinyl upholstery. The architects describe it as 'coltish'.

Above Greyfriars Court (Guthrie Photography)
Right Bargo (Branson Coates)
Opposite Cochrane Square - Wheatley House (Keith Hunter)

48

24 Cochrane Square (Wheatley House & Cotton House), Cochrane Street/Morrison Street, 1996 & 1998, CZWG

A neo-classical frontage in blond sandstone with a heavily rusticated ground floor carries on the rhythm of Rochead's deep channelled stonework on the John Street Church (see *Central Glasgow*, p.77) and the massive pilasters spanning floors one to three similarly echo the older building's colonnade. These pilasters, topped with a stone and metal railing representation of a ship's prow, establish not so much a navigational metaphor (as say, the prows extruding from the walls of older Glasgow buildings such as the Clyde Port Authority and Baltic Chambers, *Central Glasgow*, pp. 44 & 141) as one of shipbuilding. This motif is continued with the fake rivets buttoning the surface of the exposed spandrels through

these floors (1-3) and also on the soffits of the lintels.

Another interesting feature is the stylised cornice, shaped almost as a stone aerofoil. Round into Morrison Street, these two features are given a different twist with the cornices becoming a parapet on the stone-faced wings (reminiscent of CZWG's 'The Circus' in London) and the spandrels transformed into a 1950s modernist-type metal cladding.

Overheard was the following comment about the Cochrane Street frontage: 'all Bismarck's frigates breaking through Speer's façade' – *Blut und Eisen* indeed! But perhaps it's best to leave the last word to CZWG: as one of their architects commented on the Inland Revenue's choice of name for their part of the building (Cotton House is supposed to refer to the trading activities

of the post-tobacco 18th-century Merchant City): 'I suppose it's better than Slavery House!'

25 George Square

Although there has been no new building on George Square since the 1970s, the 1990s have witnessed quite a significant change in the nature of the occupiers of the existing buildings. During the decade it seems many of the large public bodies or concerns of national importance – notably the Post Office, British Gas, the City Housing Department and the Bank of Scotland – moved out to other locations. The south side in particular saw a lot of these changes and as a result there has been much refurbishment and redevelopment on that side. Among the new tenants who take the place of these old ones listed above are commercial offices, a massive shopping mall, and the Tourist Board offices.

Should citizens be asking questions about these changes, about the disappearance of civic space? And if so, where do they go to ask them now? To a telephone? To the internet? *Consumers' Advice?*

Former Post Office Building, 1875, Matheson, Robertson and Oldrieve; redevelopment 1998, Hugh Martin Partnership

When the Post Office abandoned this building and moved its central operations to the north of the city it was planned to convert it to a new National Gallery of Scottish Art and Design. In 1996 Page & Park won the international competition to design this new gallery but unfortunately the funding could not be put in place and the plans fell through. Architects Hugh Martin Partnership, who also designed **Princes**

Square, have now designed a £45m retail and leisure conversion for the building called **No 1 Glasgow**. It will have a glazed rooftop restaurant and feature upmarket retail and fashion shops. It is due for completion in October 2000.

9 George Square, 1924, James Miller; redeveloped 1998, Glass Murray Architects
The B-listed Chicago-style façades on this building were retained while the nine storeys behind were demolished. In its place a concrete frame was constructed which, in order to have maximum daylighting and a column-free interior, has floor plates organised around load-bearing central cores. The floors span 9m from the columns on the perimeter walls to the central cores in structural bays of 4.5m width. Above the seventh floor two new floors have been

created set back behind the cornice and parapet level. A new loggia has been created on the ground floor, with public access during the day and a portcullis-type motorised metal gate coming down over the entrance at night.

11 George Square, 1863; refurbishment 1996, H I MacPherson & W M Bell
The original façade of this building had been painted over, but was restored and indented with new stone as required. The balustrade at roof level was reinstated and a change in layout meant that a new entrance was required at the west end, so a replica of the east end carved portico was built at Stirling Stone's workshops prior to construction on site. New upper levels were added to the building, but stepped back with sloping lead roofs (on structural steel frames with infill

Left above Drawing of No.1 Glasgow (Hugh Martin Partnership)
Left below 9 George Square (Anne Dick)

timbers and plywood decking to take the lead covering – point of information for those concerned about the 'curse of the mansard'), so as not to detract from the façade. Glasgow's new Tourist Information and Orientation Centre is now housed in the ground floor and mezzanine and claims to be 'the largest and most technologically advanced information centre in Europe'. Inside there are murals and decorative glass panels commissioned from Glasgow School of Art and a relief frieze by Sandy Stoddart.

26 **Bar/restaurant, The Ark**, 42-46 North Frederick Street, 1998, 3D Architects
Over the last few decades there has always been a mix of trendy pubs and more traditional bars in central Glasgow, but in the late 1990s the licensed trade has seen a new phenomenon: the invasion of 'super-

pubs' run by large English breweries. Thus we have the Counting House in George Square, the Firkin in Candleriggs Market, Goose on Union in Union Street, various branches of the Hogshead chain, and now the Ark owned by Bass.

More 'corporate beer-halls' than what you might call boozers, shops or howffs, and definitely not designer bars, the most frightful aspect of this phenomenon is not the aesthetic one (i.e. more beer-bellied young men than Yorkshire, and kitsch interiors hanging with olde-worlde paraphernalia) but the anti-democratic one. Indeed, this phenomenon

represents, *tout court*, the loss of control and decision-making from the local area, and so this industry goes the way of many others before it (e.g. brickmaking, bookselling, etc.).

Even 20 years ago who would have believed that Glasgow, once a notorious centre of drinking-dens and shebeens, would become the merest branch in the boozing world. If you ask for a 'half' in one of these pubs it's likely you'll be served a completely different drink from what you'd get for the same request in a traditional bar like the Mitre, the Scotia or the Victoria (in Brunswick Street, Stockwell Street and the Bridgegate respectively – all worth a visit).

There is, however, some cause for optimism with this particular development. First, because this is new construction, not just a refit of an old building as are all those others named above. And, secondly, because local architects designed at least the shell of this building even if the interior was done by Bass's designers, Burns Design.

The 'theme' of this pub aimed at students is Edvard Munch's *The Scream*, and thus the front, rear and side elevations are all rendered in bright yellow, as part of the 'logo'. Eye-catching also is the zinc cladding around the entrance and semi-cylindrical

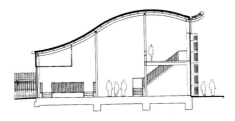

perforated aluminium screens fixed vertically to the façade, but the most striking point is the roof. A curved 'ski slope' in standing seam aluminium, it curls a wide lip out above the frontage, and brings the scale

down stylishly from a streetside 1½-storey height over the mezzanine to a single storey at the rear where thus a more intimate scale leads out to the landscaped patio area behind the building.

Inside the bar fittings and balustrading etc. in all public areas are Bass standards.

27 **Gallery of Modern Art**, Queen Street/ Royal Exchange Square, conversion 1996, Department of Architecture and Related Services, Glasgow City Council

The former Royal Exchange adds to its long list of historical functions (see *Central Glasgow*, p.88) by being converted to a modern art gallery. The pediment above the front portico flashes its message down Ingram Street with a newly mirror-glazed tympanum (by artist Niki de Saint Phalle) containing bright coloured cartoon/

Above Section of The Ark (3D Architects)
Below Detail of The Ark facing George Square with logo (Cadzow Pelosi)

surrealist images from the hagiography of St Mungo – those found in the Glasgow motto – ring, fish, Mungo, king, love, bird, tree, etc. There is no better site for a modern art gallery than the central building of a 'Glasgow Square' in the heart of the city – but this is *not* the best building. In the main room, the Earth Gallery, the boards and displays of work are an ungainly clutter in the clearly defined space under the coffered vault, and a proper viewing is invariably disturbed by the massive columns. The Fire Gallery is at basement level, Water Gallery at first floor and Air Gallery on the second. The café on the third floor with full mural by artist Adrian Wiszniewski is disappointing not least because there is no access to the roof.

28 **Buchanan Street**

Plans to make a European 'Great Street' along the lines of Champs-Elysées or Via del Corso out of Buchanan Street have existed for over 20 years, and in fact the street was first pedestrianised in 1978. Since then it had become congested with street furniture, plantings and a monstrous underground entrance, but in 1997 Gillespies, a Glasgow practice, along with Spanish firm MB.M, won an international competition to create one of Europe's great public spaces. The architects claim their design, which is costed at £10m, is of 'radical simplicity' and that it emphasises 'the identity of Buchanan Street by removing clutter and revealing the elegance of the architecture'.

Above Gallery of Modern Art from Ingram Street (Alan McAteer)

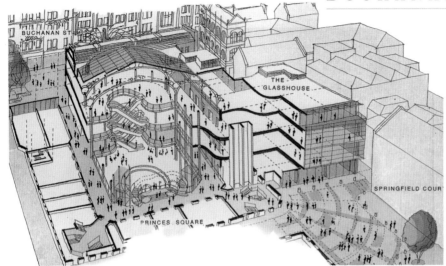

Is it just coincidence that Gillespies had already come up with a plan for this street in 1990, when they were commissioned by the Scottish Development Agency?

That plan was published in the *Architects' Journal* (May 1990) and it was there that Gillespies were the first to call for a tower to be built at the St Enoch Square end of the street. Originally the Buchanan monument, now in Killearn, was planned as an obelisk at the bottom end of Buchanan Street. A competition was subsequently organised which was won in 1993 by architect Richard Horden. His tower (which also won a competition in Zurich a few years later) is now to be incorporated in the BDP-designed

Scottish National Science Centre on the south side opposite the SECC (see pp.36-7).

The current design for Buchanan Street went on site in 1998 and phase one concentrated on creating three spaces: Concert Square, at the junction between Buchanan Street and Sauchiehall Street; Dundas Square 'to be characterised by light and movement'; and Nelson Mandela Place with a simple elegant design to 'honour the classical drama of the square and St George's Church'. The materials used include Caithness flagstones, granite, stainless and galvanised steel and strip lights in the pavements.

But is it all good news for Buchanan Street? With the completion of the Buchanan Galleries – Scotland's biggest

Left Drawing of new glass house at Princes Square (Hugh Martin Partnership)

shopping centre – it has been said that there is too much concentration of retail outlets in the one area. The George Hotel opposite the Concert Hall is undergoing demolition and façade retention by 3D Architects, to be converted into a shopping centre with the biggest Virgin store outside London; Stock Exchange House at Nelson Mandela Square is being converted to a department store; The Royal Bank of Scotland on Buchanan Street is being redeveloped by a giant American bookstore; Scottish Youth Theatre has sold its premises on Buchanan Street for conversion to a shopping centre; round the corner in George Square is the new development No 1 Glasgow by Hugh Martin Partnership, designers of Princes Square; and Princes Square itself is building a massive extension.

Questions have been asked about the viability of this concentration of commercial developments. Charles McKean has said, 'We want to avoid the city crumbling at the edges. What will happen at the west end of Sauchiehall Street and the east end of Argyle Street?' and again, on a more ominous note, 'It would be terrible if anything failed.'

29 Glasgow Royal Concert Hall,
1 Sauchiehall Street, 1990,
Sir Leslie Martin & RMJM Scotland Ltd
This building replaced St Andrew's Hall, destroyed by fire in 1962.

Plain Yorkshire sandstone cladding with classical solemnity which the latter-day addition of a glass curtain wall (1998) to the staircase facing up Sauchiehall Street does nothing to diminish. Its massive

monumentality has been described as having 'an inter-war Continental flavour' and in fact the Killermont Street frontage, with its twin porticoes and long windows, bears a striking resemblance to the Senate of Rome University built by Italian fascist architect Piacentini in 1932. The concave south-facing entrance is fronted by an open rotunda of steps (echoing the entrance stairway to Martin's RSAMD, and Mackintosh's Art School, both in Renfrew Street) and is a most successful treatment, helping D & J Hamilton's George Hotel, 1835-6 (opposite, in redevelopment 1998), wheel Buchanan Street westwards into Sauchiehall Street.

In the interior Martin has clearly sought to resolve the problem of the relationship between the auditorium and the surrounding circulation space. He has tried to get away from the typical theatre with its labyrinths of stairways and passages and to a certain extent he has achieved this by opening up wide foyers and staircases, lined in Italian marble or plain white plaster, but still there is not the feel of the cascade of

light and space which sweeps into his Royal Festival Hall (London, 1951) from the banks of the Thames.

As regards the auditorium, two major technical problems had to be solved here: first, as the auditorium sits only 18m above the

Glasgow Underground it had to be isolated by means of 450 elastomeric mountings; second, the sheer volume of the space made it difficult to attain target reverberation times (2.1 sec). Sandy Brown Associates, after intricate mathematical and electronic calculations, hung 16 fibrous-plaster baffles at precise angles from the ceiling. In 1997, however, new management removed these immediately citing the advice of 'American experts'.

Nicknamed 'Lally's Palais' after Pat Lally the Labour politician, one-time leader of the City Council, and Lord Provost, and the man most clearly identified with Glasgow's push for cultural regeneration. Is it not ironic, given Labour's monopoly of power in the city and Pat Lally's old-style leadership (there have been allegations of cronyism), that he should be associated with a building widely held to be in an old-fashioned and even totalitarian style?

30 **Buchanan Galleries**, 1998, Jenkins & Marr
Designed to complement Glasgow Royal Concert Hall, this development covers the areas south and east of the hall and over the

Above Glasgow Royal Concert Hall, north façade - Killermont Street (Alastair Hunter)
Below The Senate of Rome University (J Rodger)

top of Queen Street Station. Thus the detailing on the granite and sandstone cladding is largely neo-classical of the post-modern variety with punched-through

windows, heavy cornicing, turrets and a drum tower to the south-west corner, while there is extensive glazing across the façade to provide natural light. Inside there are two large atria linked by a glazed roof. The bridge across Cathedral Street provides three floors of glazed space and was built 'top down' with main girders at roof level and floors underneath. This bridge, reminiscent of

38 Central Station's *Hielanman's Umbrella* but with none of the latter's elegance, has been much criticised for cutting off a part of the city. Charles Prosser of The Royal Fine Art Commission for Scotland described the scheme as a 'dog's breakfast' and went on to say 'Buchanan Galleries is no better than the St James' Centre [in Edinburgh]; we

don't seem to have learned anything from our past mistakes.' *Private Eye* awarded it 'the worst new building 1998' with Piloti saying of it '... a triumph of barbarism, vulgarity, ineptitude ... '. On the Killermont Street side of the development (by Legge Ericsson), the front to John Lewis carries on the monumentalism of the Concert Hall, this time in a massive brick façade with neo-classical detailing in stone and marble, including quoins and heavy cornice.

The recessed long oriel windows break up the horizontality of the 13-bay front while the centre bay splits open the pediment. The development turns the corner into North Hanover Street with its multi-storey car park.

Above Buchanan Galleries nearing completion (Jenkins & Marr)
Right 'The Hielanman's Umbrella' after sensitive restoration by Glass Murray Architects –
part of a five-year plan to remodel Central Station (Anne Dick)

31 **Yello**, Mitchell Street, 1997, Kinnear & Crotch

Minimal but brightly coloured bar with mezzanine floor and a tropical fish tank with piranha fish. For the passer-by the large window into the lane frames the whole bar like a wall-mounted aquarium. It makes one wonder if the architects are commenting here on the behaviour of the weekend carousers.

31 **The Lighthouse** (formerly Glasgow Herald building, 1893, Charles Rennie Mackintosh), Mitchell Lane, completion 1999, Page & Park Architects

A new architecture centre constructed as part of the 1999 Year of Architecture and Design

around Mackintosh's Herald building (see *Central Glasgow*, p.100) with a new extension designed by Page & Park. The centre was awarded grants of almost £12m by various cultural bodies. It claims to be one of the biggest spaces in Europe dedicated to architectural exhibitions and has two main galleries, the one on the first floor featuring an extra high ceiling. It also has a 100-seat seminar room, education facilities, a permanent collection of its own on display, retail spaces, a Mackintosh Interpretation Centre, designed by Glasgow architect Gareth Hoskins, which has access to the Mackintosh tower and a new rooftop viewing gallery and café. Interiors are by Javier Mariscal and Sam Booth of lwd.

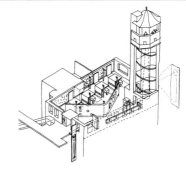

Left Yello by night (Andrew Lee)
Above Drawing of the Mackintosh Interpretation Centre (Gareth Hoskins Architects)
Below Drawing of The Lighthouse (Page & Park Architects)

32 Delta House, 48-50 West Nile Street, 1991, SBT Keppie

Massive post-modern office block with façade split into two wings both with Chicago-style long vertical windows canted out from an arched recess at the top which intrudes into the sandstone open post-modern pediments. Steel-framed and clad in sandstone with a solid granite rusticated base, on the upper floors sloped glazing and bay windows use a smoked-glass curtain-walling system.

33 Athenaeum Building, West Nile Street/ Nelson Mandela Place, 1992, HLM Architects

The former RSAMD converted to offices with basement parking. The main entrance now leads to an eight-storey atrium. On the West Nile Street façade two new floors as well as an attic have been added with post-

modern detail: keystones, cornice, arched windows and pediment. The grey metal rounded balcony which protrudes below the pediment echoes both the colour and form of Mackintosh's cupola on the Lighthouse; it is the only other circular motif all the way down this fairly dull side of the street.

34 Holiday Inn Garden Court Hotel, Renfrew Street/West Nile Street, 1995 & extension 1997, Cobban & Lironi

A French theme here allows what is basically a five-floor Glasgow tenement to show off its international relations. Thus we have the windows slightly longer and narrower than usual in Glasgow, more of a vertical orientation, a steep pitched roof, metalwork balconetti, lead-covered dormers and a corner clock tower topped by a grey dome and ship finial. It is solid enough if a bit too pastiche, but somebody must like it for £2.25m was spent on creating the extension with an extra 30 beds and sporting a canted Franco-Mackintosh type window bay.

35 **Classic House/Portland House**, 11-15 Renfield Street, 1914-16, James Miller; refurbished 1990, G D Lodge

Originally Cranston's Picture House and Tearoom with a winter garden on the roof, it was modified and then damaged by fire in 1981. Refurbished in 1990 and converted to offices, the original white faience façade, which had considerably deteriorated, was replaced by glass-reinforced concrete and the glass dome was also replaced.

36 **50/60 Union Street**, original 1853, W Lochhead; rebuilt 1994, Carl Fisher Sibbald Partnership

One half of Lochhead's building was destroyed by fire in the early 1990s and Carl Fisher Sibbald have restored the streetscape by replicating in exact details the façade, including the original balustrade. They also provided a public access pend through the building as part of the old Glasgow District Council's initiative to provide alternative pedestrian throughways across the city. The façade is in blond stone, while the pends and lightwells are in brick and render with a slightly post-modern classical flavour and some silly accompanying details like the large white urn placed in a high niche.

37 **178 Argyle Street**, 1992, Duffy, Colman, Anderson

Faced in blond stone with flimsy looking Mackintosh-style pastiche metalwork and sham top floors which are not too difficult to spot. The Union Street/Argyle Street turn is made with a drum corner above the first two floors and cheaply coloured glass in an abstract pattern. This glass is designed to operate in the reverse mode, i.e. at night it lights up from the inside to the out such that the public at large rather than the users of the building are treated to the display of colour. Unfortunately, the lights are switched off at 5pm when the workers go home! In *Glasgow Review of Architecture and Design* the critic Gavin Stamp said of the building, 'a piece of dim Post-modernism decked out with sub-sub-Toshie detail with false façade on the upper floors concealing a non-lettable void. Shame!'

Left Classic House (Guthrie Photography)

39 Foulis Building Extension, Renfrew Street, 1997, McGurn Ltd

For the brief to extend the accommodation of this squat three-storey 1960s building for Glasgow School of Art, Nick Blair of McGurn Ltd adopted two strategies: first, a new four-storey structure was built to the rear on a small area of ground used formerly for car parking; and second, the addition of a new third floor (i.e. above the ground, first and second) on top of the existing flat roof to create two large open-plan studios.

The two most interesting elements of these additions are the four-storey atrium and the new roof. The atrium is an articulation at the junction between the existing building and the new four-storey structure, which is crossed by a bridge on the first, second and third levels and allows natural light and ventilation to penetrate

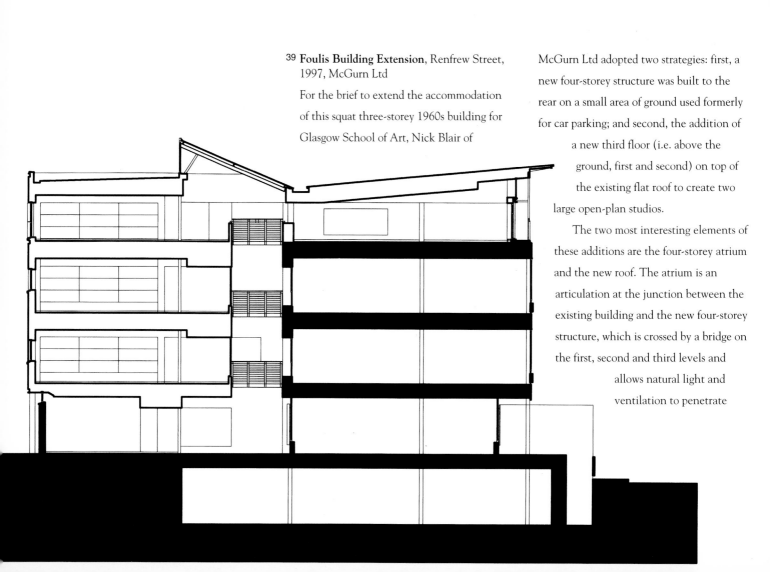

deep into the plan. The new butterfly roof is the defining component of the structure, seemingly floating above the building separated from the wallhead by clerestory glazing. The roof sails over a balcony along the front of the building and helps restore the massing and height of Renfrew Street while answering across the road to the projecting canopy of Mackintosh's roof. The existing structural bay and window rhythm is maintained on the frontage while on the side elevations the copper panels not only match

materials used elsewhere but bring home a Mackintosh-type detail on the frieze by way of Bolles Wilson's Münster Library in Germany.

40 **St Aloysius' Junior School**, Hill Street, 1998, Elder and Cannon Architects
St Aloysius' College had outgrown its accommodation in Garnethill and commissioned Elder and Cannon for new buildings on campus, including a sports hall (to be built at the Dalhousie/Renfrew Street corner) and a mathematics building (to be built at the Hill Street/Scott Street corner, pictured here). The first completed building in the plan, the new Junior School, is a purpose-built primary for 400 pupils. Most buildings of this type are low, open plan and set in wide grounds, but St Aloysius' preferred to stay in the city centre and develop the urban character of the campus.

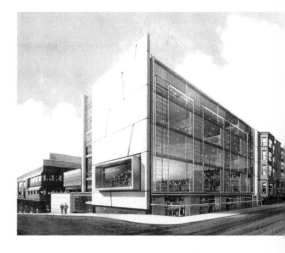

One advantage of building vertically is that it is easier to cater for security: this is seen immediately from the ground-floor plan, where visitors have to pass by the staff room, the secretaries and headmaster's office through the slate-floored entrance hall and up the stairs before they can gain access to any classrooms.

Opposite Section of Foulis Building showing new top floor and roof on existing building to front, new four-storey extension to rear, and atrium between (McGurn Ltd)
Left Copper detailing on Foulis Building (Andrew Lee)
Above Maths Building, St Aloysius (Elder and Cannon)

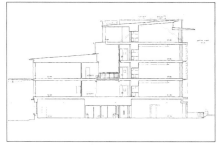

façade is fully glazed with the windows recessed behind a Terragni-style rectilinear concrete frame. Each classroom has two full windows: one with complete Venetian blinds set permanently between the double glazing at the optimum angle to let in light but avoid glare and give no distracting views of the outside; while the other window is fronted by a set of frosted-glass louvres hanging in the void created by the framing concrete box. The glazing here does thus act as a window on the street but the angles of the louvres are adjusted pneumatically (and can be completely closed down) by a solar monitor with a five-minute delay, mounted on the roof. The rhythm of these banks of

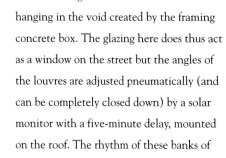

louvres along with the line of the concrete-box projection and the jutting plane of the roof overhang give the street frontage a certain cosmo-style which is certainly not out of place in Garnethill.

Inside, the classrooms are organised around a central atrium whose base is the assembly hall/gathering space on the first floor. Although the planning and layout of each floor makes them seem, in principle, indistinguishable, the architects have cleverly exploited effects of solid and void, light and shade, geometrical configurations and textures of materials to give each space its own recognisable identity. Thus on the second floor there is a high wall to the southern side of the atrium

The façades, back and front, are designed to let in a maximum of light while shielding from glare, heat and distraction from the street. The south-facing street

Above St Aloysius' Junior School (David Churchill)
Below Section of Junior School (Elder and Cannon)
Right View across atrium from viewing platform on third
floor to glass bridge on second (David Churchill)

void (over which a small child could not see) and two concrete bridges with glass bricks inset form a link to the north part of the building; on the third level there is no access to the north part of the building but a glazed viewing platform hangs out over the void; while on the way up to the fourth the slate-floored stairway is transformed into one of polished hardwood (presumably on the principle that the higher one goes, the less durable material is needed). The fourth floor also has no louvres to the street side, as it is above the concrete-box projection, but instead it is shaded by the wide overhang of the peaked roof, and gains more light from the stepped-back clerestory windows above it.

A clever and mature response by the architects for a very particular client, one feels that the children who pass through this institution will learn something about civic space, about buildings, shapes, organisation and living together. That might be an especially important lesson if most of the pupils are from the suburbs.

41 RSAMD Alexander Gibson Opera School,
Cowcaddens Road, 1998,
Boswell Mitchell & Johnston

An attempt to return to the baroque and, by implication of that style's pageantry, to a public face by an institution whose existing building covering two-thirds of this city block was described in one guide as 'dull' and 'remote' and another as 'specious' and 'meaningless'. Where the existing RSAMD (Leslie Martin, 1988, see *Central Glasgow*, p.149) on Renfrew Street and Hope Street refuses to measure up to the scale of the city grid, makes no contribution to the skyline,

Above Alexander Gibson Opera School, Cowcaddens Road (Renzo Mazzolini)
Below Section of Alexander Gibson Opera School (Boswell Mitchell & Johnston)

COWCADDENS

and uses deeply recessed fenestration to hide the body of the building behind a prison-bars-like colonnade of brick piers, this new opera school fronting on Cowcaddens Road stands in red granite cladding to the full City Improvement tenement height of the adjacent red sandstone McConnel building (see *Central Glasgow*, p.11) and continues its articulated skyline of railings, parapets and chimneys with a curved metal aerofoil.

Where the question is one of function, however, of the possibility of operating certain spaces as acoustically isolated right here in the noisy city centre, Leslie Martin solved the problem masterfully with a classical composition of a deep plan using the performance spaces as figures protected by a *poché* of dressing rooms, foyers and administration space.

Is it possible then for the Opera School, for this type of building, with its specific functional requirements, to be so 'up front' yet to remain unviolated by the public arena it seeks out? Arup Acoustics worked with the architects to form the opera studio as an isolated box, 10m high with 250mm thick walls. The studio is separated from all the other components in the building, carried on acoustic bearings. Six large triple-glazed windows allow daylight from the atrium to the studio, and the wall to Cowcaddens Road has an air space between itself and a further 140mm block and then a red Italian granite rainscreen on top of that.

Cladding above the entrance is in red Corsehill sandstone, and the colour panels on the glass walling in both the entrance and the atrium are by Art in Partnership.

42 **Piping Centre** (St Stephen's Church, 1872, Campbell Douglas, Sellars), McPhater Street, redevelopment 1996, McGurn Logan Duncan Opfer

This former church with its Italianate tower narrowly misses closing off Hope Street in typical Glasgow fashion by sitting too low under the new Cowcaddens Road, and facing south-east instead of south down the main thoroughfare. The church had been abandoned and was in danger of collapse before it was rescued by developers

Right Piping Centre interior (Keith Hunter)

The Burrell Company and converted to a national centre for bagpipe music. The new centre now has an auditorium, practice and teaching rooms, offices, a museum and library, and the manse next door has been converted into a hotel.

The most critical detailing according to the architects was the design of the practice and rehearsal rooms in the lower level of the building. They were constructed (with the advice of acoustic consultants Sandy Brown Associates) as special units isolated from the main walls of the building behind rubber supports, voids, double glazing, sound-attenuated fittings and double-leaf doors with both rubber and magnetic seals.

Original coloured glass and ornamental plasterwork in the building was restored, and new art works including a bas-relief by Tim Clark and stained glass by John Clark (of Café Gandolfi fame) have been added. The museum was designed by Lee Boyd Partnership.

43 **Challenge House**, Canal Street, 1994, McNeish Design
Smart, modern and eye-catching, this four-storey building with a triangular plan gains something of its dynamism from its orientation, sitting like an arrowhead pointing along the M8 motorway. Ideally suited to the small uncompromising site Challenge House manages to

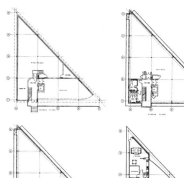

make an exciting complement out of what would otherwise be a domineering highway (and upon which most buildings would turn their backs). This steel-framed building is the most striking adherent to Corbusier's 'Five Points of the New Architecture' – pilotis, free façade, open plan, strip window and roof garden – with only the last needing room for imagination.

There is also some nautical imagery (for which the roaring traffic is heard as crashing waves) not only contained in its overall wedge shape with steelwork eaves oversailing the balcony but also in

Above Floor plans of Challenge House (McNeish Design)

details: portholes, metal railings, etc. The only downpoints are that the entrance doorway is small and quite mean for such an extravagantly shaped building and the interiors which were outwith the architect's control have been described as having 'none of the exterior's rigour or vigour'.

44 City Point, Dobbie's Loan, 1999, G D Lodge
Four-storey office block with a simple plan facing up to the motorway from the edge of the city centre. Aluminium rainscreen cladding surrounds extensive glazing, and lift shafts and escape stairs are expressed as lateral towers.

45 Malmaison Hotel, 278-282 West George Street, extension 1997, Ferrier Crawford
The plain ashlar façade of the extension with its 'Frenchy' details neatly reproduces the scale of the delicate monumentality of the pylon-doored front of the converted St Jude's Church (1838-9, John Stephen) on West George Street while round the corner it stands up to the rectilinear and larger scale of the modernist buildings on Pitt Street. The interior spaces, like the atrium

Above Challenge House (Cadzow Pelosi)
Right above Atrium between old and new buildings (Keith Hunter)
Right below Malmaison entrance, originally St Jude's (Alan McAteer)

between the old and new buildings, and the mezzanine bedrooms are interesting but the interior design lets it down.

It is strange indeed that the interior design (by Amanda Rosa) is so plush Addams Family-style Gothic, after the simplicity of the classical façade, but the point is that the whole thing is 'talked-up' too much, and ultimately seems a bit too forced and, yes, tacky.

Malmaison was the name of Bonaparte's house just outside Paris and indeed, the staircase around the atrium has metalwork railings (by Andrew Scott) which, we are told, portray the crowning of Empress Josephine. Very well, but still this somewhat flat and flimsy work gives us a feeling of 'lost opportunity' in Stephen's soaring space.

One commentator described these interiors as 'soft-slippered' – yes, the best that can be said is that they might be just the sort of 'style' loved by a certain Tory politician in Glasgow.

46 191 West George Street, 1998,
Hugh Martin Partnership

A massive corner office development with a buff polished Giallo Veneziano granite base and what the architects call a 'piano nobile' of Shuco curtain walling in tinted black glass which effectively runs through floors one, two and three. Vertical bay windows with tubular black railings running their length set up a rhythm on the street front, and the central bay has a drum tower with decorative metalwork gates set between the pillars.

Construction method was a stepped concrete raft foundation with steel frame and composite concrete slabs.

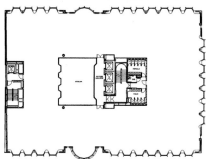

Above 191 West George Street (Paul Zanre)
Below Typical floor plan (Hugh Martin Partnership)

A five-storey atrium with rocks, plantings and bubbling water at ground level brings natural light deep into the building. Each floor, in typically modern office fashion, is column free, as the architects themselves say 'the value of modern office buildings ... will increasingly depend on the ease with which they can be adapted to changing work practices'.

The problem with this building is not just that the black glass curtain-walling with its bay windows and fixings dominates the edifice, but that it takes over the whole street and spoils the rhythm of the plain smooth ashlar fronts to Blythswood Hill.

46 **Festival House**, 177-179 West George Street, 1989, Covell Matthews
This 10m site was originally occupied by a four-storey 1930s building for which planning permission was gained to add two storeys. The architects then managed to bargain their way into planning permission for this new building, an 8½-storey Victorian-style infill with a window bay canted out between third and sixth floors above a stylised corbelled oriel window on the second floor.

The portico and corbel and soffit details are in brown granite while the rest of the building is clad in buff sandstone.

Unlike its neighbour at 191 George Street its small-sized floor plates (2600ft) and vertical stacking make it suitable only for small lets and simple users. Indeed its thunder has been twice stolen by 191, for the effect of its glass-walled elevator shaft, which looked down over a garden with a fountain, has now been blocked off by this new neighbour. Furthermore, the very pump in the lion's-head fountain was stolen while 191 was on site. The original fleurs-de-lis railings from around this fountain have now been redeployed in front of the building.

47 **Carlton George Hotel**, 44-46 West George Street, 1999, Bradford Robertson
This gap site was created after a fire destroyed the previous building. The new structure is steel framed and clad in Castle Buff sandstone and De Lank polished red granite on the lower floors. The structure of the pub on the ground floor is independent of the rest of the building, and rests on neoprene pads to prevent noise passing through the structural members to the hotel.

48 48 St Vincent Street, 1963,
Leslie Norton; refurbishment 1997,
Glass Murray Architects

Part of a project which included the refurbishing of David Hamilton's former Western Club of 1842, this programme has restored a certain prestige to this building whose white Portland stone fins should be vying in vertical emphasis with the soaring oriel bays of Nos 84-94 along the street (this latter was the first Portland stone building in Scotland).

Aside from the new vertical stack, supported on a steel structure and clad in brick, which was added to the rear of the building, several important features have enhanced the façade. A new entrance with a full-height structural grid in steel marks out the eastern corner of the building while also drawing the eyes up to the lead and steel canopy which sails over the extended sixth-floor accommodation.

49 131 St Vincent Street, redevelopment 1995,
Keppie Architects

One building with a split personality. Two separate façades here each in a version of the Chicago style. The older 1930s Grade B-listed façade which also contains the entrance to the building had to be retained while the other structures on the site were demolished, and alongside (and ostensibly

next door) a new slightly taller stone elevation was built, but tellingly, without a front door.

The façades share certain features (as well as the front door) common to the style, like the double-height plinth and heavy cornicing. Where in the older part a pilastered frontage with spandrels covering the floor plates takes up the main height, the newer has a canted bow window running this length and a balconet the full width across its extra attic floor.

The sinuous metalwork sculpture *Tree of Life* outside is by sculptor Alan Dawson, known for his metal and glasswork in Princes Square.

49 Kirkstane House, 139-143 St Vincent Street, 1991, Leach Rhodes Walker
This building has an even more schizoid character than its neighbour at 131. For not only is this one building masquerading as two, with separate façades side by side, but both these façades are designed in a hybrid of Chicago and *Mockintosh* styles. Typical of the Chicago style is the base of two storeys, with the slim main body of the building rising above towards a strong cornice.

Matters get complicated here when this main body is not characterised by the verticality of pillars or pilasters with spandrels concealing the

floorplates; but instead there are cubic oriel windows in tinted glass rising through several floors to support a balcony below the cornice. These glass boxes jutting out from the would-be elegant Chicago façades simply make the thing top-heavy.

In the double-height entry hall the Mackintosh theme is continued in a similar cheesy manner, with standard lamps as heavy-handed versions of the hanging lights in the Glasgow School of Art library, hung tapestries and stepped wall mirrors.

50 The Beacon, 176 St Vincent Street, 1998, Reiach and Hall Architects
Recognisable as work from the hands that gave us the Graduate Business School and Institute of Health Sciences (see pp.18 & 19), this building has similar features, like the Corsehill red sandstone cladding and the

Above Kirkstane House (Guthrie Photography)
Opposite left The Beacon, St Vincent Street frontage (Keith Hunter)
Opposite right The Beacon, Wellington Street frontage (Keith Hunter)

72

'low-energy, low-maintenance' ethos with solar shading of offices in anodised aluminium, with internal surfaces like bare concrete which have 'thermal inertia', and a displacement ventilation system which provides fresh warmed or cool air.

The elevation to Wellington Street is of a solid block of red sandstone with metal feature windows, while on St Vincent Street there is a variation of the Chicago style so often exploited in this street but rarely so clearly conceived. The main volume of the block takes a wedge form, recessing back at an angle from the street to leave the westernmost bays profiled like a tower, which both echoes James Salmon II's 'Hatrack' and its next-door neighbour down the hill, and gives a stop to those smaller buildings up the hill. This is presumably the 'Beacon' in question.

The Chicago theme is developed by giving this slim tower a double-height glazed entrance hall, by way of a plinth; above this rises the main body of six floors, with its manifestation here as an aluminium oriel feature, which is then topped with an oblong sculpture by Alan Johnston in a neat abstraction of the typical heavy cornice.

51 Dalian House, 350 St Vincent Street, 1990, Jenkins & Marr

The local plan for this zone of the city specified a Section 50 planning condition for the site, which means that 30% of the developable area must incorporate housing. This meant that the commercial frontage on the North Street and St Vincent Street sides of this building had to be linked to housing on Cleveland Street. The Planning Department also imposed a height restriction on the development to comply with the roof plane of the adjoining Victorian terrace in North Street.

The architects coped with these restrictions by evolving strategies to deal with the vertical and horizontal rhythms of the existing terrace. Vertical buff-coloured brick pilasters were used along the elevations with continuous long bronze-tinted double glazing between them; in this way they avoided using the levels of the separate floors to emphasise the horizontal element (these are unseen behind the tinted glass and pilasters) and so they were able to insert five floors of office space within the equivalent of four tall Victorian floors in the North Street elevation.

To emphasise and continue the horizontal elements, brick detailing in the pilasters were employed, along with the continuation of a stone string-course linking at fifth-floor level in Dalian House. There is also a link between eaves height of the buildings, with the cornice extending round the perimeter, broken only

where the octagonal pagoda-type tower rises above the corner, centring the two wings of the building. The pilastered elevation continues along St Vincent Street but suffers from a disappointing lack of 'stop'.

52 120 West Regent Street, 1990, Cunningham Glass Murray Architects

Any description of the austere classical façade of this corner office block to Wellington Street makes it sound very unusual. Yet strangely, with its rusticated bronze-red Swedish granite base forming a colonnade into the main block of pink Donnington sandstone, and the lead attic storey above the cornice, it is a very Glaswegian building. In fact, the regular rhythm of its punched-through windows has something of the classical majesty we see in 200 St Vincent Street by Burnet (see *Central Glasgow*, p.132). Its smooth façades are also an elegant modern complement to the French classical style of Wellington House next door. Unfortunately, that plain elegance is spoilt somewhat by the cheap-looking *Mockintosh* black latticework feature over the granite entrance portico.

53 Fisher House, 80 Bath Street, 1994, SBT Keppie Ltd

This corner four-storey building built around a central atrium uses a mix of materials on its façade to differing and paradoxical effects of solid and void, and lightness and weight. While the pagoda roofs step up and the cubic blocks of red sandstone mass and form a rectilinear block towards the corner from the wings of the building, and thus display a high bold monumentality, the lightness and non-loadbearing function of the stone is made clear by its hanging like a drape over the glass curtain-walling. This building performs a precarious balancing act with the Watt's art deco building on the opposite corner.

Left 120 West Regent Street (Anne Dick)
Above Fisher House (Guthrie Photography)

**54 New entrance foyer,
225 Bath Street**, 1998,
Richard Murphy Architects

A dull main entrance recessed from the street and half hidden by bushes was the problem here. Richard Murphy expanded the foyer to fill the recess and lowered the level of the floor. This way the entrance hall fronts right onto the street with double-height fully glazed windows. There is an odd contrast between, on the one hand, the vertically orientated tension of the Mies-like steel columns and the double mono-pitch roofs; and on the other, the repose achieved by the horizontal effect of the hardwood strips of flooring, and the long white orange and royal blue rendered surfaces.

Perhaps it is this contrast that makes the foyer a live space, where the rest of this building seems fairly drab. Just so, there are plans to open a café bar in the slightly raised hardwood-floored section of this space, which will 'correspond with the street life outside'.

The bank of 25 video screens by artist Ian McColl is Scotland's largest video wall.

55 Tay House, 300 Bath Street, 1991, Holford Associates

This building fills a gap site that was used as a car park for many years, and stretches one arm across the bridge to the other side of the motorway on Charing Cross. The bridge had also lain empty for years, was considered by Glaswegians a planners' mistake, and dubbed 'The Bridge Too Far'.

This bulky new building in salmon-pink cladding mounted on a brick wall plinth with grey metal pillars supporting and strip windows round the façade, turns away from Sauchiehall Street, and ultimately the city, by orientating its corner entrance on Newton Street/Bath Street to the M8 motorway.

The entrance hall is floored in stone and marble and the walls covered in shipbuilding murals. This entrance and the other

Opposite Entrance foyer, 225 Bath Street (Paul Zanre)
Left above Structural detail of interior (Paul Zanre)
Left below Section of entrance foyer (Richard Murphy Architects)
Above Tay House at Bath Street/Newton Street corner (Anne Dick) *Below* Tay House (Anne Dick)

'extremities', like the stairway to the bridge on North Street, and the drum corner to the east end at Bath Street have mirrored glazing, as if at the ends of the building these points are bursting out the pink skin.

Building over this site has not, however, put an end to the controversies; not long after it was built the then President of the RIAS caused a 'stooshie' when she remarked that a certain terrorist organisation should plant a bomb in it.

56 Eagle Building, 215 Bothwell Street, 1992, SBT Keppie

This elegant glass tower, with its geometric massing and its twin elevator shafts soaring like glass turnpike stairs 11 storeys above the street corner, stands as a modern-day tower house guarding the edge of the financial district.

Steel-framed with glass curtain-walling and rainscreen overcladding, in the three-storey entrance hall it houses a reconstructed part of the original Eagle Building sandstone Venetian façade to two storeys with full cornicing, keystones and arched window details. The façade is wrapped over and around the stairway to the mezzanine so that it acts as a stone veil, and thus, oddly, the older building (1854, by Alexander Kirkland) is an intriguing supplement to the newer, giving a delicate touch to what might otherwise seem grim high-tech.

As an insight to the point of view of the planner, Keppie Architects tell of a comment made as the plans passed through the various committees towards planning permission. The building could not be considered overly

tall for that site, said one official, because there is 'no view down Pitt Street anyway, because Pitt Street is one way'.

In *Ulysses* James Joyce has his younger protagonist define Irish Art as 'the cracked looking-glass of a servant'. Might we not

follow the greatest urban poet by defining the planner's art as 'the diminutive rear-view mirror of a suburbanite'?

57 **Alhambra House**, Bothwell Street, 1997, G D Lodge

This massive post-modern style, neo-classical building with art-deco overtones takes up one whole block (where the former Alhambra Theatre stood) and stands up to the powerful Renaissance façade of the Atrium Court opposite. An imposing building with a wealth of articulate detail: heavy bracketed cornicing, turrets at the corners, columns, generous glazing and metal spandrels.

Built as a reinforced-concrete raft foundation supporting a steel frame with suspended *in-situ* concrete composite floor slabs. Reconstructed stone and granite clad

Left Eagle Building entrance hall (Keith Hunter)
Above Alhambra House (Guthrie Photography)

precast concrete panels are fixed to the perimeter structure. The cladding panels are made of Giallo Bras-Lucido granite imported from Italy, and as the main elevations have such complex stone detailing, stepped in both the vertical and horizontal planes, mouldings were prefabricated from reconstructed stone to complement this granite cladding.

The architects say it would have been too costly and time-consuming to use traditional masonry construction for these details. Ultimately, however, it must be suspected that it is this prefabricated element that gives the building a somehow too shiny, plasticky look – ought traditionally crafted details like this to be mass-reproduced in this way for instant style? The strict modernist would say that this sentimental attitude (i.e. of the supposed innocence of applied detail) is simply a measure of hopelessness. But then, we are all post-modernists now – or is it post-post-modernists?

Then again, can any citizens really expect to find hope in the façades of buildings in the financial district? Yes, if they look at the rear of this building hidden away in the service lane they will find a smooth ashlar front with a light classical flavour and none of the oven-ready detail. What a pity.

58 **Anderson Centre** (1967-73, R Seifert Co-partnership), redevelopment (now renamed **Cadogan Square**), 1997, Holford Associates
The Anderson Centre, a 1960s vision which integrated commercial and residential property in a single megastructure, with car

Right above Cadogan Square (Guthrie Photography)
Right below Cadogan Square, interior of entrance pavilion (Guthrie Photography)

parking, services and a bus station all under a deck carrying shops and offices, and around three tower blocks of flats, is undergoing a 'regeneration'.

The bus station has been removed and the decks and megastructural details are being smashed away from around the tower blocks and offices. In this way an urban streetscape is being recreated, with streets, gardens and squares – Douglas Street has now been reconnected to Argyle Street for the first time in 30 years.

Holford Associates have completed phase one of the plan: Cadogan Square. Two glass-walled drum pavilions have been built as entrances to the existing office blocks,

with green-panelled oversailing roofs supported by outlying pilotis. Between these ends of the development on the Douglas Street/Cadogan Street corner a landscaped rock garden with a pond has been set out.

Richmond House, 20 Cadogan Street, 1991, Holmes Partnership
The strict geometry of this glass cuboid makes it appear strangely weighty. Eight storeys of blue reflective glass sit on a plinth of Kemnay grey Aberdeen granite.

59 **Fitzpatrick House**, 18 Cadogan Street, 1991, HLM Architects
Eight floors of offices decked out with classic 1980s post-modern details. Flimsy stylised pediment forms and, of course, the oriel windows in classic Cadogan *Mockintosh*.

60 **Princes House** (formerly Magnet House, 1963-7, Leach Rhodes Walker), 50 West Campbell Street, redevelopment 1998, Fletcher Joseph
A dull office block which fronted onto Waterloo Street reoriented onto West Campbell Street in this redevelopment. The new frontage is a pavilion sitting upon a

Left Richmond House (Anne Dick)
Above Princes House (Guthrie Photography)

green and silver granite podium with a glass and silver aluminium envelope and an oversailing roof. The top storey has been removed and there is a new more interesting skyline, but the stepped-back elevation to Waterloo Street is still pretty dull.

61 Centre for Contemporary Arts refurbishment, 336-356 Sauchiehall Street, Page & Park Architects

The largest grant ever given by the Scottish Arts Council will fund the plans for the CCA to expand into adjacent properties

and create more diverse and flexible exhibition and performance spaces as well as new cafés, bars and retail developments.

Page & Park's plan seems to be to highlight the fact that the CCA is housed in not only one building, but almost a city block, and in particular that it is an Alexander Thomson building: Grecian Chambers.

It is appropriate that one organisation rooted in the city should be identifying itself with, and trying to create a new 'brand' image (CCA) for itself around this building, as almost alone among Thomson's commercial work this building is not only a façade, but turns a corner (into Scott Street) and so has a greater depth and solid individuality while still belonging to a continuous urban fabric.

62 Berkeley Square, Berkeley Street, 1998, Davis Duncan Harrold

This red-brick building is a replacement for a distinctive block, described as a 'misplaced provincial schloss' (see *Central Glasgow*, p.171) which had, over the years, been the subject of many redevelopment schemes. Abstracting from the traditional city closed four-storey tenement block around a central courtyard, this design sites a three-storey hipped-roof pavilion at each corner, which not only recreates the monumental public face to the street and fills the city block, but

Above Princes House entrance hall (Paul Zanre)
Right Section of Berkeley Square (Davis Duncan Harrold)
Opposite Berkeley Square (Andrew Lee)

82

also nods at history by reminding citizens of the previous occupant.

The rhythm of the brick colonnades and large tinted-glass windows takes the streetfront gaps between the pavilions in its stride so that the continuity of the street wall is ensured, and these gaps are turned into gateways opening the raised courtyard to light, air and unexpected views. Thus a protected urban space is created which has an austere classical feel under the eaves of the pavilions.

63 Glasgow Caledonian University

Originally a technical college, this institution was raised to the level of a university in 1993. Most of the original buildings on campus date from around the 1970s and were orientated in a quite typical introverted modernist fashion towards an internal square, turning their backs to the city. Since 1993, however, there has been a new masterplan and several new buildings have been, or are being, built.

These buildings appear to be making an attempt to be a part of the city. The architects involved are talking about giving 'definition to the edge of the campus on North Hanover Street' and creating 'a new entrance to Cowcaddens Road'. Land engineering contractors are building a 'grand avenue' and a 'piazza' with a stone

gateway which leads from Cowcaddens Road into a public space between the three main new buildings: the library extension, the health faculty and the sports building.

Materials have been chosen carefully – like the Corncockle red sandstone – to start a 'dialogue' with the city. The problem is that this institution and others around have turned their backs on the city for so long, that it now appears there is no city to face up to here. Cowcaddens Road has only the low back of a bus station opposite the university, and on North Hanover Street there is no urban frontage at all. Another problem is presently being created inasmuch as the new Buchanan Galleries building is acting like a citadel wall and cutting off anything to the north and east of it from the centre.

Britannia Building, 1996,
Keppie Architects

Designed in the classical French manner this irregular-shaped building presents urban

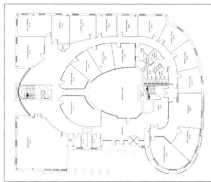

Right above Britannia Building, Cowcaddens Road elevation (Keith Hunter)
Right below Ground-floor plan of Britannia Building (Keppie Architects)

84

façades on two sides (south and west) and a plan arranged around the central figure of a courtyard, with rooms distributed according to a hierarchy of public/private function. Indeed there is a continuous play here in both material and form between the private and the public, and the traditional and the new.

The northern elevation, away from the city towards the campus, is an elliptical form, clad in glossy white Neoparies panels (it is the first time the Japanese molten-glass

material has been used in this country) with smoked-glass windows. Taking the nautical metaphor to the bridge, the architects say it makes references to 'Glasgow's shipbuilding heritage' and also, that with the heads of departments' offices here in the round, 'the shape of their rooms allows these "captains" a panorama over the university campus'.

As it is not a completely public building open to all the students (it houses the departments of risk & finance, finance accounting, and university management group) the entrance is half concealed cleverly at the eastern point where the red sandstone façade meets the glass screen walling, behind sandstone pillars and masts.

It is unfortunate that this building is stranded in the modernist desert of the Caledonian University Campus, for with its

two traditional red sandstone frontages ('hard edges to the campus') – one stuck behind a lawn and railings onto the dismal Cowcaddens Road, the other looking over some sort of car-park slip road – it is ultimately an urban hôtel *sine urbe*.

Faculty of Health, 1998, RMJM
The university has the largest health faculty in the UK, running six academic departments: biological sciences, nursing and community health, psychology, physiotherapy, social sciences and vision sciences; and thus this project is seen as one of its most significant.

A concrete-frame building with aluminium cladding built to cater for a varied and complex set of functions, the architects have worked with the same

Left Britannia Building, northern elevation (Keith Hunter)

engineers as worked on Reiach and Hall's health science building at the University of Strathclyde (see p.19). Again the design team has worked here to create a low-energy building, with similar features such as concrete walls left exposed where possible to take advantage of 'thermal inertia', and aluminium shading and walkways protecting the southerly-facing Velfac curtain walling from sunlight.

Another technical problem was posed by the building's proximity to Queen Street Station: the labs had to be isolated acoustically by constructing one room inside another with the inner resting on top of dense rubber acoustic pads.

The seven-storey block running north/south carries some detail – trellises etc. – on the top floors reminiscent of Richard Meier's work, while the drum-like floor plan of the south-facing part gathers the visitor into the main entrance.

William Harley Library extension, 1998, Austin Smith : Lord

The original library was constructed in the 1970s, and this extension to the east is separated by a 3.6m glazed gap with link bridges which allows light into the deep plan.

The building has a reinforced-concrete frame with coffered slabs supported by cylindrical columns, and cladding is in pre-tensioned silver-coated aluminium rainscreen.

The new entrance to the complex, a triple-height structurally glazed box with a

Above Faculty of Health (Andrew Lee)
Right William Harley Library extension from Cowcaddens Road (Austin Smith : Lord)

86

steel and glass staircase, helps in the reorientation of the campus back towards the city by facing onto the new grand entrance plaza opening to Cowcaddens Road. Ground-level elements and also the pier motif from the Britannia Building are carried on here in the same red Corncockle sandstone, as though this bright new metallic techno future is rising out of the red sandstone frame of traditional old Glasgow. A metaphor for Scots university education here?

Sports Hall, 1999, Wren Rutherford ASL
The sports centre completes the creation of two new public spaces sitting across from the new library extension to close off the 'square' which is the entrance from Cowcaddens Road, and forming the south wall of the east/west running 'avenue' by sitting

opposite the Faculty of Health.

The double-curved roof, clad in aluminium panels, is a strong expression of

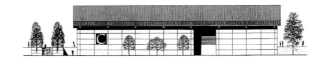

the functional organisation and asymmetrical plan of the building (it accommodates two multi-use sports halls – total floorspace 3500m²), and also projects the whole campus boldly out towards that 'hard edge' on Hanover Street.

A fully glazed two-storey entrance foyer mirrors the new library entrance and provides lift circulation for the disabled to move up from the lower level square up to the avenue. External materials are sandstone and silver metal panels, again matching the effects of those on the library extension.

87

Above Elevations of Sports Hall (Wren Rutherford ASL)

64 The Galleries, Sauchiehall Street/ Argyle Street, 1989, Cooper Cromar
This blond brick gushet building metaphorically bats the ball back across the tennis courts of Kelvingrove Park to the art gallery and university spire with the boast – *anything English Goths can do, Scottish po-mos can do better!*

The six-storey square tower on the gushet acts like a gateway to the city from the west end, and keeps up the scale of the neighbouring tenements but with a plethora of post-modern detailing: leaded dormer windows, pediments, heavy cornicing in stone, rusticated ground floors, a step-back balcony floor and some Glasgow-style metalwork.

On the rear side to Argyle Street a study in solid and void, with slightly deconstructed post-modern details; including suspended gardens, a cubist peristyle on a high terrace and blue columns supporting balconies above the void that is the entrance to the underground parking.

65 Housing, Byres Road/University Avenue, 1994, Simister Monaghan
This housing infill was built on the 15m-wide gap left when University Avenue was connected through to Byres Road forming a new crossroads with Highburgh Road. The end gable of the tenement where the avenue had been smashed through was left skinned in buff brick. So the architects have built the Byres Road frontage up to the regular four-storey height, but then in order to step

round into University Avenue and down to a three-storey height, they have at the same time made a roof terrace of the corner block and terminated the Byres Road block there with a pedimented gable pavilion opening onto the terrace.

The University Avenue elevation sweeps up the street with a bookend stop and start, both topped by parapets, while in the central section overhanging eaves penetrate at regular intervals. A stepped section through the building has meant that there are four storeys facing the rear, while onto the front opposite the University Avenue terrace are the classical three storeys.

66 **Glasgow University Library**, 1997, extension Holmes Partnership

It was decided to extend the building upwards, creating a new floor, as this would avoid problems of separate buildings and remote storage of stock. The reinforced concrete frame of the existing building was built on piled foundations so there was no trouble with the extra loading of another floor.

A new glass curtain wall with a bluish tint has therefore been added between the brutalist towers, and a metal standing seam

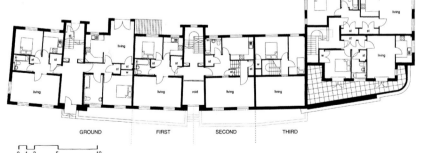

GROUND   FIRST   SECOND   THIRD

0 1 2   5   10

Left above Housing in University Avenue (Simister Monaghan)
Left below Plan of housing showing different layout on each level (Simister Monaghan)

roof with a curved central section and cam-shaped aerofoil features at the eaves to deflect air movement.

The problem is that the smoothness of these new features diminishes something of the crude vernacular-style Italian hill-town effect achieved by the towers. There is also a new double-storey height fully glazed Meieresque entrance lobby.

67 Gilmorehill Halls (originally Anderson Free Church, 1878, James Sellars), Bank Street; conversion 1997, SBT Keppie

A Grade B-listed church transformed with the help of the Scottish Arts Council Lottery Fund into the new Department of Theatre, Film and Television Studies for the University of Glasgow.

The plans to include a cinema, theatre and rehearsal spaces, as well as television studios and sound-recording booths, research facilities, teaching areas and offices, meant that the floor space had to be expanded from 1500m² to 3200m². Thus seven new levels were created in the massive stone shell of this Normandy Gothic church.

The existing floors were removed and in the new space (23m high) between the basement and the underside of the roof trusses, a steel structure was slotted in, infilled with acoustically engineered plasterboard and glass.

Of special interest is the theatre on the fifth level, nestling below the original stencilled, timber-panelled ceiling and with natural light from the original leaded-glass windows. A 'trampoline' lighting grid has been installed – the first of its kind in Scotland.

The theatre foyer stretches to the full height of the building and is lit by the 9m-high stained-glass window.

68 Great Western Road/Belmont Street/Clouston Place Housing, 1997, Elder and Cannon Architects

This complex of private and public housing and main street retail units combines a practical complement to the urban fabric with interesting and unique features which contribute to the 'character' of the area. In terms of the complement, each of the three façades has to face up to totally different streetscapes: on Great Western Road the smooth ashlar monumentality is given a horizontal emphasis by the ribbon windows over the shop fronts and the rhythm of the heavily corniced fenestration above. Further chimes with the period effect from Miller's weighty Jacobean style across the road (see *Central Glasgow*, p.193) are gained from the tourelle at one corner and the boxed oriel window jutting out at the other.

The building steps down into Belmont Street after a classic-scale brick tenement with a double-height glazed lobby, and a series of stone fins, which appear capped by the roundel copper windows projecting from the roofs, blend to the scale and elevation carried up the street by the existing Georgian terrace with its dormer windows.

In Clouston Place, the tenement scale is preserved with a neat effect of terrace gardens suspended over the void that is the pend leading out from the off-street parking in the back court.

As for the characteristic features, a screen wall, set at an angle to the Clouston Place/Great Western corner and supported on pilotis above the shop-front, faces boldly across the Kelvin Bridge, and acts like a massive stone gateway to the West End.

Meanwhile above this sits the squat tower, in standing seam copper with a flattened-out elliptical cupola, clearly an attempt at contemporary development in the tradition not only of Miller's across the way, but Mackintosh's in West Nile Street (see p.59).

69 Office, 382 Great Western Road, 1997, Anderson Christie Architects

Stylish office on two floors, basement and ground, plus mezzanine, converted from

Above Exterior of Anderson Christie office (Kevin McCourt Photography)

M & A Brown's bakery. The tenemental shop-front has been given a chic makeover, with two minimal keep-out black-tinted rectangular windows and industrial metallic fixings and door which give it an air of secrecy, mystery and the underhand.

Inside, however, all is bright and welcoming, with yellow, cobalt and scarlet walls. A section of the ground floor immediately behind the façade has been removed, so that on entering one crosses a bridge from the door over the void down to the basement, looking deep into a brightly coloured meeting room.

Past the bar/reception are the offices to the rear with original features of the deep bakery oven, white-glazed brick walls and the full-height arched windows which bring light up to the mezzanine.

The user of this building is rewarded with something of the 'Tardis' effect – the unexpected is always pleasantly in your face, in terms of colour, volume and perspective.

70 **Great Western Court**, Maryhill Road/Great Western Road, 1998, Cooper Cromar
A question for the Glaswegian socio-architectural critic would be: what distinguishes the gushet from the merest corner? Something to do with the angle at which the two streets meet, no doubt. This six-storey corner block of flats with the widest chamfer in town seems to lay open the question. The brick façade, with stylised stone-screen and pilasters, echoes the west-facing portico of Clarendon Place (see *Central Glasgow*, p.192), while the angle and massing of the stone wall are reproduced once more further up Great Western Road at Elder and Cannon's Clouston Place corner (see p.91);

Above Interior looking down into basement (Kevin McCourt Photography)
Below Interior view from mezzanine to rear (Kevin McCourt Photography)

but by then the columns have completely disappeared into the void and all we have is a vertical strip of windows down the ashlar facing.

Thus did the orders die on the Great Western Road.

Left Great Western Road/Clouston Place Housing (Keith Hunter)
Centre Clarendon Place (Keith Hunter)
Above Great Western Court (Keith Hunter)

REFERENCES

Bibliography

P Carolin & T Dannatt, **Architecture, Education & Research**, 1996; A Dunlop & F Sinclair (eds), **Bringing the City to the River**, 1996; K Frampton, **Modern Architecture**, 1980; Tom Gallagher, **Glasgow: The Uneasy Peace**, 1987; M Glendinning (ed.), **Rebuilding Scotland**, 1997; M Glendinning, R MacInnes & A McKechnie, **History of Scottish Architecture**, 1997; J Hendry (ed.), **Chapman 78-79**, 1994; James Joyce, **Ulysses**, 1922; J Kelman, **Some Recent Attacks**, 1992; J F Lyotard, **The Postmodern Condition**, 1984; J Macaulay & C Hermansen (eds), **Macjournal 3**, 1998; Charles McKean, **The Scottish Thirties**, 1987; C McKean, D Walker & F A Walker, **Central Glasgow**, 1989; Francisco Sanir, **The Münster Library**, 1994; T C Smout, **A Century of the Scottish People**, 1986; Ian Spring, **Phantom Village**, 1990; G Walker & T Gallagher (eds), **Battle Hymns & Sermons**, 1990; E Williamson, A Riches & M Higgs, **Glasgow: Buildings of Scotland**, 1990; Young & A M Doak, **Glasgow at a Glance**, 1965/71.

Acknowledgements

Special thanks to Professor Charles McKean for advice and criticism, to Helen Leng and Susan Skinner at the Rutland Press for patience and encouragement, to Eilidh Donaldson of the RIAS for enthusiasm and vital assistance with research, and to Raymond Burke for reading through the manuscript.

All the photographers and artists accredited in the book have been most generous in providing images. Not only do their contributions make this guide something special, but without them it simply could not have been.

Neil Baxter Associates are to be thanked for the use of their map, and Jon Jardine for his time and skill in preparing it for us.

All featured architects have been most prompt in providing invaluable information and illustrations, and many others have helped in ways too numerous and convoluted to mention, but they know who they are; they shall receive a personal acknowledgement.